Praise for Elaina Zuker

"Elaina Zuker has written a clear, concise and helpful book on moving out of stagnation to setting and reaching your goals. She has some smart ideas on peer mentoring and easy to use suggestions for identifying skills and goal setting. The book is written in accessible and easily understandable language – as exemplified by the title itself.

You X 2 is for anyone who is looking for ways to turn opportunities into reality. Elaina draws out a very clear path for the reader to follow to understand how to get the most out of collaborating with a partner and exchanging ideas, thoughts, experiences and skills to get things done. This book is a must-read for anyone who is juggling many tasks and wants to focus on important goals."

— Dr. Leslie Faerstein

℘

"A QUICK READ FOR GOAL ORIENTED SUCCESS! This is "it" if you are looking for a well-focused and concisely defined quick and lively read. You will easily connect to your own personal needs and goals as you strive for the success you deserve. Go for it!!!!"

— Emily Rosen, Author and Writing Coach

℘

"I read it from cover to cover and just loved it. It was interesting, factual and easy to grasp. In my over thirty-year real estate career I have worked in partnerships and "mentoring" relationships with many other professionals and to mutual benefit. For some of them it would have been useful to have had Elaina's model and "contract" ideas to clarify those relationships!"

— Janet Gifford, Realtor

"In this new, compelling book the author has articulated a practice I have been doing instinctively throughout my long career in staffing and management consulting.

Assessing a candidate's skills and client's needs and making a "perfect match" is essentially the art she describes in this fascinating and practical volume about how to create a strategy for achieving any goal.

I highly recommend this book to anyone who is stuck moving forward to their goals. In fact, buy two, one for you and one for your future peer-mentor."

– B. Heiken, Executive Search consultant

"I think you really want this book, if you have serious goals and want to go after them the smart way. This is not one of those 'you can do it' feel-good books. This is a clear eyed, clear-headed guide to today's workplace and how to navigate it swiftly and directly with the help of a peer mentor. In addition, Ms. Zuker has taken the time to help you find exactly the right buddy for your specific "buddy-system" needs. All of the how-to's are carefully charted for you. How to plan. What to expect. How to reciprocate. Ms. Zuker has also taken the time to think everything through so precisely that you don't need to take much time to read it (although it is a pleasure to read). *A Powerful and Practical Book*"

– N. Miller, Advertising Executive

"This informative business book provides the reader with some unique ideas for increasing your business success through the sharing of skills...it is a skills bartering system that can be of huge benefit to small business owners and start ups. Barter is ages old and has been used in many different ways throughout the ages. Elaina's research and the input of colleagues, offers the reader some great ideas on how to leverage your skills in order to gain some that you may not have or wish to learn.

Any business owner will find this approach worth the read and possibly worth exploring to improve outcomes and even bottom lines!"

– Sandy Chernoff, Business Consultant

⁂

"A brief but informative guide to navigating the new, sharing economy and how to form learning partnerships for business success."

– Barbara R. Block – Management Consultant

⁂

"Elaina has written another practical and powerful book to help get better results in the business world. As an owner/operator business, I sometimes wish I could have a coach or a mentor by my side to guide me, offer me the skills I don't have and motivate me to get going on my next project or make that difficult phone call.

I especially liked the "Skills Inventory", the Goal Setting exercises and the "how to" details she provides. I've already started on my search for a Peer Mentor.

I recommend this book to anyone wants to advance their career and build lasting relationships with smart and interesting people."

– Marcia, Media Consultant

⁂

"As a strategic planning business consultant, I see many mid-level managers and executives who operate alone, and without the support, feedback and encouragement so necessary to their success and mental health.

I especially liked Elaina's simple and powerful model of Peer Mentoring in this excellent and user-friendly new book. The wonderful descriptions, charts, exercises and Skill Assessments help to shorten the learning curve for any busy person to implement these ideas and put them into action right away.

The chapters on the anthropological and historical roots of barter and sharing practices stirred my interest as cultures drive performance. Working with corporate anthropologists and strategists, organizations see the importance and impact of Peer Mentoring and mutual support in groups, teams and departments.

I recommend this book to anyone wants to advance their career and build lasting relationships with smart and interesting people."

– Molly Sutherland, Business Consultant

☙

"I read this book after I heard Elaina Zuker speak at a workshop in New York City. The idea of peer mentoring was new to me. This book is a breeze with a thought provoking premise. Elaina points out that as we intuitively and organically move more and more towards a sharing economy, the individualistic "by my bootstraps" ideology/myth has run its course and we are starting to be more honest and explicit about the fact that we rely on a network of friends and contacts for our successes.

Elaina takes it a step further by providing a very practical guide to how professionals can create explicit, one-on-one peer relationships that can propel them towards their mutual goals through an equivalent exchange of expertise.

Before meeting Elaina and reading this book I was in an informal peer mentoring relationship where a friend and I promised to encourage each other on our career development paths. I was pumped and energized and moving ahead very deliberately with my goals. Elaina describes all the processes and rules to help make the journey successful. I am ready to explore a peer mentoring relationship now. Thank you Elaina. ***Peer Mentoring Works!*** "

– Shindy Johnson

☙

"Elaina and I have been in a high-energy, focused, Peer Mentoring relationship for several months, and I can say that it has increased my motivation and productivity exponentially. We set our telephone appointments for every 2 weeks, for a specified amount of time, state our individual "desired outcomes" for the call, and I emerge refreshed and re-energized with lots of positive energy for my projects.

As a solo-entrepreneur, this type of support is so valuable to me; Elaina has truly tapped into an important need we all have, and in her compact but power-packed book, has given us a user-friendly technique for you to put into action now! Buy two – one for you and one for your Peer Mentor! The Skills Inventory Gave me Great Insight"

– JB, Author and Consultant

"I found this book to be very interesting, thought provoking and constructive as well as instructive.

I have never been much of a team player but this book gave me a different perspective on how to achieve or heighten success by benefiting from the skills of a peer mentor.

Although I was not aware of the term " peer mentoring " I now realize that I am in a similar relationship with a colleague of mine but without any actual written or oral contract. I am her mentor in my field - real estate - in which I have many years of proven experience and success. As I continue to guide and advise her, she is of great assistance to me with her technical skills (which are far superior to mine) and helps me to save considerable time on technical and administrative tasks.

I enjoyed the chapters on barter, gift giving, potlatch, and the kula ring and learning how these early forms of doing trade developed and led to our business practices of give and take today.

I thought the author did a great job of describing these early practices to put into perspective a modern-day "system of barter" in which individuals can help each other professionally without any monetary exchange.

What really left its mark on me was the chapter on *skills inventory*. I found it both well thought out and intriguing. 4.0 out of 5 stars! A unique approach to gaining new, beneficial business skills."

– Real Estate Broker

YOU X 2

PEER MENTORING IN THE NEW VIRTUAL WORKPLACE

ELAINA ZUKER

Copyright 2021 © Elaina Zuker
www.ezinfluence.com

ISBN: 978-1629671697 (Paperback)

All rights reserved. No part of this book may be reproduced in any form or by any electronic or mechanical means, including information storage and retrieval systems, without written permission from the author, except in the case of a reviewer, who may quote brief passages embodied in critical articles or in a review.

Trademarked names appear throughout this book. Rather than use a trademark symbol with every occurrence of a trademarked name, names are used in an editorial fashion, with no intention of infringement of the respective owner's trademark.

The information in this book is distributed on an "as is" basis, without warranty. Although every precaution has been taken in the preparation of this work, neither the author nor the publisher shall have any liability to any person or entity with respect to any loss or damage caused or alleged to be caused directly or indirectly by the information contained in this book.

Cover design by Paula Laniado
Produced by Brian Schwartz for Wise Media Group

v428

To Nadav – The Spirit of Generosity

Contents

Praise for Elaina Zuker I
Introduction 13
1. The Peer Mentor System: A Relationship Model Whose Time has Come 15
2. The Difference that Makes the Difference 21
3. What Does WFH Really Mean? 27
4. The Gift: Rituals of Exchange and Contract . 31
5. The Sharing Economy – Making a Living, One Gig at a Time 43
6. The Peer Mentor Model: A 21st Century version of an age-old practice 52
7. Barter: How many Cows for That Smartphone? 63
8. Peer Mentor: A Unique Partnership Characteristics and Comparisons 70
9. Goals 76
10. Skills Inventory 92
11. How and Where to Find a Peer Mentor 102
12. The Agreement 106
13. Communication Skills for Success with Your Peer Mentor Contract 109
14. Peer Mentor Progress Assessment 113
Conclusion: The Beginning 118
Also by Elaina Zuker 120
Acknowledgements 124

INTRODUCTION

Today's workplace is rapidly changing. So much so, that employers, employees and the self-employed need to thoughtfully consider their options when it comes to global forces that can disrupt and permanently alter the course of doing business. Virtually every business sector across the world is being turned on its head by forces such as the gig economy, consultants, work for hire temps, work from home employment, as well as, social distancing, epidemics and now even pandemics. Some of the biggest challenges that corporations and small businesses will face today are; maintaining productivity levels, preserving communication structures, and stabilizing morale, especially when employees are forced to work from home due to unforeseen global issues. All of these issues can be addressed and greatly alleviated with a Peer Mentoring program; one that is designed to produce impactful results even with just a few employees or throughout a large organization.

First or all, you may be wondering what a title like *You X 2* really means? It sounds a lot like an amazing rock band. What it really refers to is, the many studies that show how better results (often so much better) are accomplished and greater success is achieved when two people work together. As an employee at a corporation, a small business owner, or as a single business operator this can mean getting an exponential increase out of one of the most important resources – you – and most often, the costs of these greater results are minimal, or next to nothing! Bringing two colleagues together to support each other, (three when necessary, if there's an odd number in a smaller business) can have many outstanding benefits when wrapped around the framework of Peer Mentoring - which can be done either face-to-face, or, virtually.

If you want to increase your productivity, enhance your earning power, achieve your goals, and reach more overall success in your life, whether measured monetarily, in expertise, or through your personal or professional relationships, then read on. Peer Mentoring is a system in which two people agree to support each other based on complementary skills and needs, and the partners create an "agreement." The purpose of this process is to create a productively paired 'buddy system' to help likeminded career partners achieve corporate or individual goals.

There have been many books and articles written about mentoring, finding someone senior to you in your field that will help, advise, consult, and coach you to realize your potential. Having a mentor (if you can find one) can definitely be an asset to you and your career. Lately, we hear a lot about the power of networking in all its formats, such as 'live' networking – go-to events, collecting business cards, and then following up on those contacts. Of course, we also have some terrific cyber networking platforms thanks to social media networks such as Facebook, Twitter, and the most business-focused platform, LinkedIn. The end goal is finding the contacts that will be helpful to you, your career, or your business. Peer Mentoring is a combination or convergence of these two trends (networking and mentoring); regardless of the business or career you're engaged in.

My goal in writing this book is for you to not only find the idea of a Peer Mentor intriguing, but most importantly, that you will find that it's a practical and powerful way for you to achieve your goals!

1.

THE PEER MENTOR SYSTEM: A RELATIONSHIP MODEL WHOSE TIME HAS COME

I first discovered how beneficial and valuable Peer Mentoring was when I began using it for myself. I met another consultant who had many of the skills, experiences, and contacts that I lacked. I had some of the resources and talents she needed. We formed an agreement with each other where we made very clear statements of our individual goals, and then made clear written commitments to support each other in achieving those goals. Some of this support came from teaching each other the skills the other needed, sharing our contacts, educating each other in areas where we needed more information, and, most importantly, just knowing that we each had a buddy rooting for us. Our mutual support system was so effective; we found that we both achieved our one-year goals after only a few months. During this period, we met once a week, reviewed our short-term and long-term goals, discussed how effectively we were spending our time, and took turns instructing each other on subjects in which one of us wanted more knowledge. We were so amazed by our success that we decided to teach this process to others. Now, thousands of people all over have learned the process and are actively forming Peer Mentor partnerships to help each other become more successful.

Peer Mentoring is a process through which people identify their own resources, and those of others, and then create specific strategies for mutual goal achievement. It is a new adaptation of the age-old concept of reciprocity practiced by all cultures. Usual reciprocal practices are implicit, whereas a Peer Mentor agreement makes the arrangement explicit. The participants then barter resources (skills, contacts, technical expertise, advice, counseling, criticism, etc.) with each other as needed. That idea alone sets it apart from the plethora of 'how-to-succeed' theories. This model encourages the development and organization of one's readily available resources – personal, business, and social – and is based on mutual support. It is different from the "I can do it myself through gritted teeth" attitude, which I believe most people find extremely difficult in real life. The Peer Mentoring technique challenges the myth that isolation is a necessary companion of success.

Peer Mentoring is based on a complementary and balanced relationship that offers many benefits for its participants. The value in these exchanges is that they are not necessarily about friendship, having a good time together, or even being similar in respect to their personal career objectives. In fact, the agreements often work better when there are differences – complementarities – between the partners. Each peer is then both the mentor *and* the protégé. Complementary skills and needs form the basis of this system of pairing. The pair becomes a relationship for support, guidance, and resource-sharing to achieve each individual's goals.

As an Influence expert, consultant, bestselling author, speaker and corporate trainer, I have run seminars and workshops with groups around the world on topics as varied as Influence Skills, Writing Skills, Time Management, Leadership, Team Building and Peer Mentoring. At the end of the workshops, participants are organized into complementary pairs, and are then shown how to use the Peer Mentor process to reinforce what has been taught.

In the case of the Influence seminar, participants assess their strengths and weaknesses within that skillset, and the Peer Mentor Agreement serves to reinforce those skills after the workshop. The workshop on Peer Mentoring itself, is much shorter, and focuses entirely on the why, what and how of forming Peer Mentor partnerships.

The partners are instructed to spell out clearly what they want, what they are prepared to offer each other and then put all of these details in writing. This process has proven to be effective in many settings: at the manager, staff, and entrepreneurial level, as well as in schools, colleges, and non-profit groups. Numerous workshop participants have asked me for further advice on how they can adapt these techniques and the methods, implementing Peer Mentoring into their professional lives; which led to me write this book.

The Peer Mentor relationship is not wishful thinking nor is it hard to do. In fact, many have told me how easy it is to implement and to put into regular practice. It is structured around a written agreement between two people which specifies in detail, what goals each person has, what strategies will be used to achieve them, the targets, timeframes, measures, metrics, and indicators by which they will know when the goals have been reached. The operative word is "peer;" that you find someone at your own level to work with and preferably not a senior or superior person in rank or position. This way there will more-or-less be a balance in what you can offer each other. The role of the Peer Mentor is to keep the other on target, to help push through the fears, internal blocks, and procrastination – to believe in the other, even when they do not believe in themselves. It's just like having your own personal coach, morale booster and accountability partner.

Each participant must agree to both receive and provide the support, counsel, sponsorship, and advice that will be designed specifically for each agreement. Each agrees to an exchange in what both parties consider to be a fair trade. The partners must be explicit, describing clearly what they expect of each other and how they will know when they are living up to their ends of the partnership. The feedback they give each other will focus on being objective, positive, and specific. When appraising the behavior or activities that appear unfavorable or off target, each Peer Mentor needs to deliver the feedback as constructively and specifically as possible, focused on the behavior and not the person. Suggestions for improvement are requested, not given without solicitation. Each partner's goals and objectives are spelled out clearly and explicitly, so each knows what the other means. Then, each partner designs strategies or activities to achieve those goals with specific indicators to measure success: "how will I know when I'm there?" The goals are the "what" – the strategies are the "how."

Your Peer Mentor's role could take a number of forms. For example, one partner may be more politically savvy than the other and might help you figure out which projects would get you the most visibility and recognition in your organization. Your partner may help you understand how to influence your supervisor or others who have some say over your career and salary review. Similarly, your Peer Mentor could help you rehearse a discussion you have scheduled with your boss. If you are in business or run a professional practice for yourself, your Peer Mentor could help you with your sales technique, financial planning, or advertising strategies. The Peer Mentor model is based on the idea that the partners have an investment in and commitment to each other. There will undoubtedly be conflict, diversions, and distractions at times, but this is perfectly natural in an intimate and committed relationship.

I'll explain the concept of Peer Mentorship more fully and give a historical and anthropological overview of similar practices in various cultures through the ages. I'll also explain how to find a Peer Mentor to achieve important goals in any category in your life. I'll show you ways to measure your success as the Peer Mentor relationship develops, how to select the best person to work with on your agreement, how to set realistic goals, how to create an actual Peer Mentor agreement and how best to communicate with your partner.

THE BENEFITS OF PEER MENTOR RELATIONSHIPS FOR A CORPORATION OR ORGANIZATION

For corporate employees, the benefits of Peer Mentoring will especially become clear and noticeable within a short period of time. Technology has evolved so rapidly, to the point where employers now have a significant number of staff and temporary contract workers working remotely from home. Peer Mentoring will particularly help here in terms of keeping staff engaged while simultaneously relieving managers who may not be able to be as involved with their staff as they no longer work in close proximity with them.

Using the Peer Mentor model encourages the professional development of individuals within a corporate or organizational structure. It economizes and wisely uses the existing human resources of a department or the whole organization. The process promotes esprit de corps, because of the mutual support aspect of the concept. It moves people from the attitude "I don't need help, I'll do it myself" to "I have a great resource, a bank of people I can turn to for assistance".

Peer Mentoring is a superb way for managers to utilize staff with strengths in one area to help improve the abilities of staff who might have weaknesses in that category of skill. This is a big departure from managers who don't want to invest the time to help improve an employee. It is good business to support people in their self-development, teaching them the simple processes, and then giving them ongoing support.

For example, here are the basic steps a corporation or organization might use:

1. Invite managers to an Executive Briefing on the Peer Mentoring process
2. Conduct a two-hour seminar with employees, walking them through the processes of Setting Goals, identifying Skills and Resources, finding a Peer Mentor, right then and there, followed up with the creation of a Peer Mentor Agreement.
3. Conduct follow/up support meetings with the pairs periodically. Monthly, every three months, etc., via live sessions, or videoconference calls.

Participants share what they have learned, as well as the benefits and challenges they have faced. These findings are summarized and shared with the group, as well as the managers.

The benefits to the organization as a whole have been described as:
- creating an environment of learning, improvement
- promoting a value system of helping colleagues
- avoiding job burnout and routine-fatigue by offering challenge, versatility

2.

THE DIFFERENCE THAT MAKES THE DIFFERENCE

Sometimes, what you're missing is <u>the</u> important ingredient for success!

There's a big problem in the world of career advancement today. Even though we may be competent, educated, smart and ambitious, somehow our big goals elude us. And for others who may be more advanced in some respects, the more difficult it can become to admit that there are big gaps in our skills repertoire. When you're the division manager, it's hard to ask for help. The last thing you want is to appear as if you lack confidence and expertise in a certain area and that you actually may need some help.

So, you "tough it out", "fake it till you make it", or whatever you tell yourself you have to do. But there's still something nagging at you. "If only I could understand how that system works. But who can I ask? I'm supposed to know this by now."

Imagine that you had a "guardian angel" who could fill you in on the information you're missing, or don't understand, or wasn't included in your technical training for this job. Wouldn't it be nice to know there was someone in your corner who was committed to helping you, who you trust, contributing to your success, without judging you or without ulterior motives?

Here are some lucky (and resourceful) people who found just that:

Kayamisha, a branding and marketing consultant landed a $400,000 project with a large publishing company. The work would take months and require several printed components.

Kayamisha had never managed such a large project. She would have to arrange for a letter of credit from the bank to pay the printers and other vendors.

In the meantime, she was so preoccupied with getting this project done in time for the client's deadline that she was neglecting her other clients.

She didn't have the required experience to manage the finances for something this complicated. Moreover, if any of the printed projects were not perfect, she would be responsible, having already paid the printers with the bank's line of credit, and would have to re-do it at her expense.

A week earlier, at a networking meeting she had met a woman, Meredith, who was an accountant and financial advisor. Meredith had mentioned that she needed help with some sales materials for her practice.

Kayamisha contacted her, and they sat down and made a short-term agreement to help each other with their separate challenges. Kayamisha, confident she could trust Meredith having checked out her reputation and long standing relationships with loyal clients, got some good advice about managing her cash flow. Meredith got some tips on creating her sales brochures.

※

Jorge was an ophthalmologist who had graduated from his university program with honors, and had worked in the ophthalmology department of a major teaching hospital.

After several years, he decided to begin his own practice, sell beautiful eyewear and open a shop. The only drawback was that he had no experience in retail store design or merchandising. Many of his existing patients followed him to his store for eye exams and to purchase new glasses.

But the shop didn't look very exciting or trendy; the window wasn't catchy-looking enough to attract the fashion-forward clientele he was seeking to buy high-end designer eyewear.

Joann, an interior designer, had just arrived in New York and was introduced to some Hispanic new clients there. But her Spanish was rusty at best, and most of the affluent Spanish speaking homeowners she was being introduced to as clients required at least a modicum of Spanish conversation to feel comfortable with the designer. Jorge was fluent in Spanish; so the two worked out an agreement where Joann would help Jorge with his store and window design and Jorge would help Joann get her Spanish up-to-speed for her new clientele.

∞

Brenda had just been hired as the top legal counsel for Levi-Strauss, in San Francisco, one of the oldest clothing manufacturers in the country. Although the company had been around "forever"- they were one of the pioneers in many new forms of management – they embraced "ad hoc teams", "MBWA – Management by Walking Around" and the flat, rather than hierarchical organizational structure.

Brenda had come from a large, very traditional and undemocratic law firm and left because her goal of getting promoted to partner seemed unlikely.

What she found at her new post though, was her complete unfamiliarity with the style and norms of how the company functioned. She was used to the "top down" way of managing. So, when she held her first staff meeting, one after another, the attorneys in her department asked questions, made suggestions and didn't wait for her to "lead" the meeting. They had been trained in the much more "democratic", participative style, which was now the norm in the company.

Brenda realized she had to act fast. She approached Haley, an acquaintance who was a therapist (for groups and individuals) and asked her for coaching in "listening" and "facilitating" meetings. Of course she knew her desire for confidentiality in this relationship would be honored; as a licensed psychotherapist Haley would respect the therapist/client relationship.

What did Haley need? She needed legal advice to help her with a lawsuit in Small Claims Court which wasn't really worth enough to hire counsel, but she still needed some sound, yet basic help to help her strategize her case.

ೞ

Kiaria, who had been working in the paint department of a big box home improvement store, had seen an increase in purchases of specialty paints, largely due to the improving construction market.

She decided to strike out on her own, and open a specialty paint store in her town. She knew all about the products, and was great at advising customers.

The challenge she was running into, though, was finding, screening and managing the employees and subcontractors she would need. Painters are sometimes outside of the mainstream employment market; many are competent and responsible, while others seemed to be less disciplined and could sometimes be tardy.

Kiaria asked Raphael, who owned a reputable moving company for advice on this matter. Movers have similar issues when hiring staff and contractors.

Raphael was flattered to be considered an expert, and when he thought about it, he realized that Kiaria had a skill that could help him. He asked her for suggestions on paint colors and brands to use to paint his moving trucks.

Their exchange of skills was not as formal as a Peer Mentor relationship, but Kiaria was able to address the main "gap" in starting her new business.

As we shall see, there are many such examples of hurdles and challenges in businesses and careers, but now there can be a solution if you a) recognize what's missing and b) are resourceful in identifying someone who has what you need.

From time-to-time, all employers and small business operators face unforeseen and significant revenue shortages and also miss their profit targets. For employees, this can be an opportunity to show your worth and shine. This is something that freelancers, consultants and entrepreneurs, have likely figured out already on their own in the course of conducting business. And this is where Peer Mentoring comes in - to help us all work together to achieve better results and "take it to the next level".

Peer Mentoring takes practice and may take a bit of time and effort to become accustomed to. However, it can become the "glue" that brings people together. Peer Mentoring promotes those great feelings of pride, camaraderie, and reliability that are shared by individuals and groups, teams and task forces that may now be working remotely.

So what exactly do you have to share with your colleague? You might believe that you have nothing of great value to offer to anyone. But truly, if you really stop and think it over, it's not too hard to see that we all have something that we can share. There is more about this later in the book, but here are just a few thoughts to give you an idea of what you can share to get you started. And don't stop here! Feel free to add to this list as it's only here to give the notion of Peer Mentoring tangible meaning to you.

SKILLS INVENTORY – THE PRACTICAL AND SPECIFIC

Before you begin your Peer Mentor Agreement you need to assess your specific skills and resources while also identifying what you would appreciate receiving some help with from your partner. Just to get you thinking now, here is a mini Skills Inventory list you can use as a way for you to begin identifying your key resources (or "gifts") that you are willing to offer and also those areas where you would welcome your new Peer Mentor's input or support.

Later, you will get to the part in the book where you create your own skills inventory – you will be compiling the list of skills you can bring to the table. And, you might be pleasantly surprised when you see all the "gifts" and talents you have to offer!

Skills I Can Offer or Want to Receive:

Dealing with People
- counselling
- teaching or leading
- negotiating
- delegating

Dealing with Tasks
- assembling items
- producing things
- using equipment
- writing

Dealing with Data
- computer issues
- analyzing data, working with spreadsheets
- designing research study
- organising data

The actual lists (detailed later) that form the skills inventory are longer and more detailed – the skills noted here are meant as a sample to get you thinking about where your strengths are and what you might need help with. This "Assets and Liabilities" inventory is then summarized, so it can be shared with a potential Peer Mentor to determine if there is enough of a complementarity to make a match. The Peer Mentor Partnership Agreement can then be negotiated, once you have a clear idea of what you actually have and what you want/need.

3.

WHAT DOES WFH REALLY MEAN?

At first, the thought of **working from home** (WFH) or remote working, even just temporarily, might sound really great. It's like having an indefinite number of snow days, without having to lift a shovel! Some can honestly say that they just love remote working. But staying put after a few days, or even weeks, is somehow quite a bit different. Working from home is not all about, sleeping in, reading novels and streaming movies or shows. So how does Peer Mentoring play out in regards to working from home? I truly believe that Peer Mentoring is even more relevant in this situation as working from home can get lonely after a while. Working from home often comes with the feeling of isolation, a potential decrease in your passion for your work and so many different distractions - I think I just heard the cat scratching at the door to get back in - and never mind all of the truly wonderful and some of the absolutely time-wasting videos that one can check out and watch on YouTube or on your social media accounts.

So that you can be effective and productive at your job, as well as a competent Peer Mentor, here are some things that you will need to prepare for, when working from home. Some days, there isn't going to be a proper beginning or end to your workday. For others, such as those in the Tech Industry who have wonderful lunches provided for them at work, they are now spending time lingering in front of their open refrigerators wondering where the sushi is or maybe where those really nice burritos are going to come from.

Working from home can be really convenient for some, and totally inconvenient and disruptive for others. The global threat of an epidemic, or even worse a pandemic, can force nearly everyone to be plunged into a disorienting territory when you have to work from home all of a sudden. Maybe your household is actually not as cheerful a place as your office environment. What happens when you find yourself now being forced to spend more time with family members who you may not be getting along with that well? I sincerely hope that's not the case for you, but in reality, it's an unfortunate fact of our times. Others will really miss the social aspect of an office environment. Missing out on talking at the water cooler or in the lunch room, about "the big game" last night or a terrific new movie that you just saw will be a great loss of social camaraderie for many.

You will also need to think about setting up a proper and private home workstation. Do you have something you can use as a desk and do you have an appropriate place to put it? It's most ideal if you can carve out a place where you won't be constantly interrupted or distracted. Maybe you also have to consider your young children that are also now unexpectedly at home from school. Do you have a comfortable chair? Do you have sufficient Internet bandwidth? And do you even have all of your passwords and contacts collected somewhere so you can access them remotely when needed?

Another important thing to ensure is that you have a suitable video communication space. Video conference calls are much more common now and essential for some, and they need to be operated efficiently and effectively, especially if you are the host of the call. Video conference calls are really useful when speaking with your Peer Mentor. Eye contact, even if it's just virtual eye contact, is truly important when you are trying to help each other. It's important to be aware of the background that you have behind you, especially if your room is a mess. I was once on a video call and the person on the other end had some pretty offensive pictures on the wall in the background. Today there are some really attractive and creative backdrop scenes available that hide the unmade bed that is really behind you. And sometimes for fun, or if you haven't brushed your hair today, you can even replace yourself with a meme. Video conferencing software is readily available to help with this.

Tele-Conferencing and Video Tips

Before you make a tele-conference or video call, make a test video call where you can check your audio and video settings to hear and see if there is any unwanted background noise or visual issues. If you will be joining a video business call with a colleague, or going on a team meeting, I highly recommend doing this test video call first as that will eliminate the sudden stress of getting on a call, only to find out that you have voice or video problems. Simply schedule a meeting and invite someone, maybe your new Peer Mentor. This will help remove any issues with your headset or webcam that might arise when tele-conferencing with a customer or colleague.

If you are using your webcam for your meeting, think about de-cluttering your office space before getting on video. Also, "clean" your screen before a meeting. This means that you should close all other open windows and applications unless they are related to your meeting. When screen sharing, ensure that you are only presenting what you need to. If you use the "enable preview" function for incoming email messages, you will want to make sure that this is disabled, otherwise everyone you are sharing your screen with will see your email messages as they come in.

∞

Once you check to make sure that you have sufficient Internet bandwidth to handle working from home, you really need to make sure that you refresh all of your passwords regularly and make sure that you use strong ones to prevent hackers from breaking in. This is an unfortunate consequence of our times. Many don't realize how insecure their home internet connection is, compared to the safe VPN protected environment that they typically conduct business from. Cyber security experts warn us to be on the lookout for fraudulent, well-crafted email messages that pretend to be offering information about health or business concerns. ID thieves do not take a break and can be very creative. No matter how good these messages look, (they will likely contain some valid information) be especially cautious of clicking on any links these messages may contain. Be careful to not let your guard down in this area especially.

You also have to set some simple boundaries for yourself, so that you don't fall into a trap, or worse, fail to keep up with your work. If you have more than a thirty-minute commute, then maybe you can think about adjusting your alarm by that amount of time to catch a few more *Zzzzzs*. However, it will likely help most of us to just keep your alarm set for the same time as usual, put on the coffee, eat breakfast, take a shower and get dressed. Ultimately, just do everything you would normally do as if you were going into an office setting. You may want to consider putting on your jacket and taking a walk, to the park and back for those thirty-minutes, to get a little fresh air. It's essential to start your day off on the right track, especially when working from home.

I'm also a big believer of keeping the TV off during your work hours. Some swear that they can multitask and even focus better with it on. It's true that some sound, even just ambient sound, can be better for most than a totally quiet room. I recommend putting on some low-to-medium-key music, and the good thing here is that you get to pick it! I often work best with some classical music playing in the background. Then when I break for lunch, I'll switch to the news.

Every morning is a fresh start. I begin sorting my plans for the day in my head and then jot out some of the most important things that I want to cover for the day. There's no doubt that it will be a rare day when you will get everything on your list done, but I find this simple approach really helps me focus on the most important tasks to be accomplished. Obviously, other unexpected tasks or interruptions are going to pop up that will require your attention, even mundane things such as, paying bills, going on errands or a knock at the door from a neighbor or friend. That's alright, cut yourself some slack. Take care of these things, and then go back to your list to keep yourself on track for the day. Taking a few moments each day, to review your top one or two daily objectives with your Peer Mentor will help you accomplish so much more. Even if you just send a text or email to each other of your top daily goals, you will find that your focus will be clearer and that that you'll check a lot more off of your list.

4.

THE GIFT: RITUALS OF EXCHANGE AND CONTRACT

Dr. Gabriella Djerrahian
Assistant Professor, Sociology and Anthropology

Every year during the holidays, Christmas rolls around with a mega-frenzied shopping spree. Before I go any further, let me just get the deed done. I admit it. I'm one of *them*, a middle-class shopper who spends ridiculous amounts of money to buy presents for other middle-class recipients who really don't need them. Yet, every year, I find myself running amok from one shopping mall to the next, trying to come up with original gift ideas that will somehow outdo or, at the very least, equal what I gave last year.

None of the awesome presents I buy, buy, buy are for me - at least not at first glance. Like other holiday shoppers, everything I purchase is, well, to be given away. Now, before we start patting ourselves on the back in approbation of our infinite generosity, let me remind you that by the time New Year's rolls in, my pile of give-away presents has been replaced by a new pile of gifts that others bought expressly for me. For one thing, the gifts we let go of come back to us through highly ritualized exchanges - gifting and counter-gifting - in the commercial hoopla we call Christmas. So why go through the trouble of just moving stuff around from one person to the next, year after year, in a never-ending cycle of reciprocity? The answer is quite simple: gifting is a ritual that consolidates bonds between friends and families. It makes us feel good to show people we love just how much we care. And, yeah, I feel like a five-year-old kid when I open my presents. It's just plain fun.

We tend to think of rituals as the exclusive purview of tribes or ancient societies, the clichéd image of Native American men sitting in a circle on the floor, decorative headgear and all, passing along a pipe and exchanging presents with their white counterparts. Gift giving as a form of ritual, however, is alive and kicking in our modern, urban lives, and Christmas is not the only time when we participate in it. A few years back, a dear friend of mine announced that she was getting married. In the same breath she forbade us, her besties, from throwing her a bridal shower. This request did not go so well with mom-in-law-to-be. What do you mean there won't be a bridal shower?, she quipped. "Throughout the years," mama explained, "I have attended and given gifts at so many bridal showers, it's your turn to receive now." Her reaction clearly demonstrates another aspect of gift-giving based on rights and obligations: the right to collect what is 'due' to the new family into which my friend was marrying and the obligation to fulfill the role of both the giver and the receiver. There is also the issue of honor wrapped up in this. Letting others return our gifts to mark an important rite of passage in a woman's life, as marriage has traditionally been, allows the giver the opportunity to honor kin the same way that we have honored others in the past.

The idea of obligation in the form of gift giving is seldom mentioned out loud in our society. Nobody advertises Christmas as an opportunity to "buy more so you can get more." How selfish would that be? These anecdotes, however, underline the circulation of gifts and the untold obligation to return (and, in the last example, to receive). This ensures the circulation of goods that go around as presents. Cultural norms are crucial for determining who gives, who receives, what the goods circulating are, and how and when exchanges take place. Why do we continue to invest so much time and energy to perpetuate the gift cycle?

This is one of the questions that inspired the brilliant French sociologist Marcel Mauss (1872-1950) who wrote about it in his seminal essay called "The Gift: The form and reason for exchange in archaic societies," published in 1925. Almost a century ago, Mauss showed that what the gift does – the function it serves – is far more important than the actual gift itself. What power resides in the object given, he asked, that causes its recipient to pay it back?[1] To answer that, he delved into historical cases of gift giving, solidarity, and social relations in ancient civilizations and tribal societies.[2] This isn't to say that Mauss' own society had no role in his intellectual trajectory; on the contrary, Mauss wrote about the gift because he was inspired by rapid changes unfolding around him in twentieth-century Europe. Social inequalities and economic crises were increasing, and the push towards individualism in the wake of mass industrialization propelled him to think about the role of solidarity in emerging political and economic systems.

THE POTLATCH: A "TOTAL SERVICE"

Of the various gift-giving practices that Mauss described, the *potlatch* captured the imagination of generations of readers and came to epitomize the essence of his book. The potlatch is a complex gift giving ceremony institutionalized by some Native American communities along the Canadian and American North-West Pacific Coast. While varieties existed in the way that potlatches were structured, Mauss drew from the general idea of the potlatch and highlighted a common feature: the competitive gifting and counter-gifting ceremonial feasts that occurred within the framework of hospitality and rivalry. In extreme cases rivalry between opposing tribes led to combat, violence and even death. Let's call this more dramatic category of potlatches "extreme gift-giving."

For Mauss, the potlatch is nothing more than a system of gifts exchanged, or, as he called it, a "gift economy." To put it simply, a chief would throw a huge party for a bunch of tribes. The objective of the ceremony would be for him to show off his high social standing by giving away his wealth (gifting) in a way that competed with the guests' ability to do the same towards the host (counter-gifting). The word potlatch itself has been translated into "giving" (in Chinook), or "to give" (from the Nootka verb "pa-chide").[3] In some cases, showing off not only meant redistributing one's wealth according to the donor's assessment of the receiver's worth, but its sheer destruction as well. The elites' title of chief was put to the test based on how much they were able to get rid of by gifting or destroying, following a period of accumulation for the purpose of potlatching.

Not all potlatches were of this combative – or agonistic to use Mauss' term – nature. Moreover, it wasn't only about huffing, puffing and oversized male egos. People feasted, gifts circulated, and alliances were made and broken. Titles and, accordingly, social hierarchies were re-assigned. Outdoing one another through the act of giving away wealth was orchestrated by rituals that took place within a highly complex legal and political system.

Mauss used information gathered by other scholars to put together his analysis of the potlatch. He consulted documents written by people who witnessed first-hand how the tribes mentioned in *The Gift* used to live. These accounts were largely collected from the late 1800s to the early 1900s when colonial interference and European domination over native populations started to bear important changes in the potlatch. *The Gift* was written at a time of massive transformation and cultural loss for these communities. For Canadian authorities, the potlatch represented one of the most important obstacles to killing off native cultures and "taking the Indian out of the Indian."[4] In their quest to "civilize" Canada's indigenous population, the government banned the potlatch between 1884 and 1951, making it a legal offence. The destruction of valuable objects like copper only reinforced their objective to kill off the potlatch once and for all. Authorities could not wrap their heads around the act of deliberately getting rid of one's own material wealth through its annihilation. It countered the very idea of the capitalist society Euro-Americans were so keen on building. In our society, one attains success and fortune through the accumulation, and not the distribution, of wealth. The potlatch represents the polar opposite. Now, for those of us too eager to evoke the tired, romantic idea of the altruistic and selfless "noble savage" who is really about peace and sharing, Mauss offered a powerful antidote. The purpose, it seems, of giving away wealth was to gain more in the form of honor, power, and prestige. Once again, Mauss showed that gift giving is really a system of exchange and that gifting is not a random act of kindness, even in the case of the potlatch.

The potlatch touched upon every aspect of life in the communities where it took place. For this reason, Mauss considered it a "total service."[5] The concept of total service also alludes to the fact that the chief was the combative mediator who gifted and counter-gifted his clans' wealth on behalf of the collective as a whole. Through his study of the potlatch, Mauss argued for a more holistic, or "total," approach to the gift because the potlatch represented a religious, spiritual, economic, juridical, and social affair that mobilized all aspects of a community. Though the act of gift giving is conducted by an individual giver to an individual receiver, person-to-person gift exchanges take their symbolic cues from the collective framework of relationships between groups. In the context of the potlatch, gifts were not anonymous objects but rather, had their own spirit imbued with the identity of the giver and of the larger group to which they belonged.

THE KULA RING

Mauss spent an important part of the book introducing another gift exchange circle found among natives of the Trobriand Islands called the *kula* in what is today Papua New Guinea. His analysis is based on information he gathered from anthropologist Branislow Malinowski, who spent years doing observations in the region starting from 1914. Malinowski was stuck there due to the outbreak of World War I and could not return to Europe. He spent hours observing the kula, among other practices. The kula ring refers to a large exchange network in which goods moved between islands and communities. The two most valuable trade commodities were armshells and necklaces, which circulated in different directions. Whereas armshells moved counter-clockwise, necklaces were traded in the opposite direction.

Malinowski wondered why people would go to so much trouble, at times navigating dangerous waters from island to island, in order to maintain a circle of exchange of non-utilitarian goods. The observations he reported about the kula clearly demonstrated that the natives of the Islands were indeed capable of rational thinking. Attributing the capacity of rational thinking to the Islanders went against the general notion of the day that equated 'savages' to 'backwardness' and a lack of intelligence. Instead, Malinowski argued that the kula is a highly complex gift economy that is really about political authority. Items traded did not have a utilitarian use but they had social, political and spiritual value. Both armshells and necklaces represented social status and were part of a much larger system of exchange that included useful goods such as food, hospitality and in some cases, women. Mauss considered the kula to be the extreme example of a larger, more general network of exchange within and between tribes.

Once again, as with the potlatch, Mauss applied the principle of the kula to unveil the idea of a contract in regards to gift giving. The contract of the gift goes against our general assumption that gift giving is a voluntary act divorced from interest, reciprocity and expectations. The examples of the kula and the potlatch show us that what appears to be at first glance gift giving in its purest form, in other words without strings attached, is actually linked to interests and obligations that regulate spiritual life, economy, kinship and political alliances between giver and receiver.

Like Malinowski who applied the example of the kula to demonstrate that natives were actually rational-thinking beings, Mauss' study of the gift offered a commentary on the capitalist ideology of wealth through accumulation by presenting both the potlatch and the kula as an alternative to the capitalist market. In western societies we consider that more, more, more translates into wealth and success. For native communities who practiced the potlatch, wealth was translated into the value and prestige of what one gave away or expedited through destruction. Doing so was a direct reflection of the value and prestige of the giver's worth and social standing. Contrary to the logic of the capitalist market, the goods exchanged within the gift economy were not about maximizing economic and material profit.

In eighteenth- and nineteenth century European thought, the native had been revered as a 'noble savage' not yet polluted by the obligations of a modern life. Whatever romanticized notion of the 'noble savage' as altruistic and selfless beings that Rousseau and others portrayed evaporated with Malinowski and Mauss' works, among others. Keeping tabs, being selfish, and wanting more (more wealth to keep as possessions or more wealth to give away and get more prestige) were just as alive and well in "tribal" communities of the past as they are in our own society. What then, is the difference between exchanges of goods as commodity and exchanges of goods as gifts?

GIFT AND COMMODITY EXCHANGE[6]

Economists and social scientists have long thought about what constitutes a transaction of goods and services between two parties. What makes an exchange commercial in nature? How are economic transactions different from the exchange of gifts and counter-gifts? Let me begin by giving a play-by-play of some of the key ideas that economists and other scholars have considered in thinking about the difference between commodity- and gift-exchange.

According to Mauss, there is a difference to be made between gift exchange, as described in the examples of the potlatch and the kula, and commodity exchange. He believed that the economy of small-scale societies such as the Trobriand Islanders and Native American communities like the Kwakiutl revolved around gift exchanges. At the heart of the distinction between both types of systems is the quality of social relations. In the gift exchange, people are reciprocally bound even after the transaction is complete, and there is a high level of interdependency between both parties. The receiver continually holds an obligation to the giver and vice versa, leading to a circular flow of exchanges that insures the maintenance of long-term relationships. What determines the value of goods exchanged is not their economic value, but rather their social, spiritual, political, and symbolic worth. In these communities, the gift forges alliances, bringing people together in a dance of giving and receiving, giving and receiving, giving and receiving. Essentially, the function of the exchange was to uphold a moral purpose. Moreover, the goods being gifted were thought to be imbued with life. Gifts carry their own spirit from owner to owner.

In commodity exchanges, the basis of capitalist societies, the transaction occurs between two parties, often strangers to one another, who engage in trade or barter. Social relation is not a precursor to the transaction, nor is it necessarily something that the transaction gives rise to. The obligation to return and the moral concerns prevalent in gift exchanges are not primary considerations. Economic value of the commodity prevails in all other aspects, and it lacks in "symbolic uniqueness." The idea of profit and economic rationality are central tenets of commodity exchange. This, of course, is not to say that gift giving ceremonies like the potlatch and the kula did not abide by their own economic and calculated logic of exchange, but that the purpose and the means of those exchanges varied significantly from commodity exchanges, among other differences. As we saw in the example of the potlatch and the kula, self- and collective-interests are guiding principles in gift exchanges. Others point out that the main difference between gift exchange and simple barter is the lapse of time between the act of giving and counter-giving.[7]

What is interesting in terms of peer-to-peer mentoring is that exchanges in the form of gift giving are not so different from trade or barter in that rationality, self-interest and economy characterize both transaction types. Exchange is really about reciprocity, whether the cycle of gifting and counter-gifting comes full circle on the spot (during Christmas, for example) or at a later time and place (during birthdays and other occasions).

Let's bring back the potlatch ban for a minute. It's quite safe to say that the practice of destroying valuable goods, particularly copper, goes against every fiber of our hyper-consumer ethos. If we take a closer look at our own Christmas gifting carnival, it's not hard to see how the expenditure of thousands upon thousands of dollars each year is, well, kind of silly. I'm not bringing up this point to suggest that we should stop gifting or showing appreciation to those we love by way of presents. What I am pointing to, however, is that the way we do this is through commercialism, and that this is very much a symptom of the consumption-based societies we live in. Of course, there are alternatives to status quo gifting practices, yet none of them have gone mainstream. For one, we could make our own gifts, but then again, who in their right mind would do that? Imagine having to make gifts every time your child had a birthday party! Just the thought is enough to make a working mom go crazy. Another option would be to re-gift, lest we be labeled a "re-gifter" like in the Seinfeld episode in which Jerry received a label maker from the dentist Tim Whately, only to discover that Elaine had originally given Tim that same gift. Tim's outing as a re-gifter who recycled the label maker was anything but a compliment.

One of the more important concepts we can take away from Mauss' *The Gift* is that pure gifts do not really exist, whether in small non-Western communities or in large-scale Western societies. Systems of exchanges, be they gift- or commodity-exchanges, share many characteristics (economic calculation, self interest, obligation to return, etc.) and are based on a common principle: entering a contract. A contract binds two parties to an exchange in which details have been thought out and agreed upon prior to accepting the agreement. Implicit contracts are the basis of our economic functioning. When I happily overpay for a cup of frappa-mocha-slightly-warmed-up-lattucino-with-non-soya-soya-milk, I hand over my money to the cashier fully trusting that he or she will deliver, whatever hilarity might ensue about the fluffed up names we now use instead of "coffee."

These contracts are verbal, while others are written and/or legally binding. The peer-to-peer mentorship contract discussed by Elaina in this book is a great example of non-monetary transactions. I suspect that Mauss would gladly re-think some aspects of his book in light of the way goods and services are being exchanged today.

PEER-TO-PEER ECONOMY: "WHY BUY WHEN YOU CAN BORROW"?

The collaborative economy, as the sharing economy is also called, is booming in Canada and the United States. There is a movement of regular citizens who are doing away with possessiveness and making accessible what they own. Cars, homes, beds, sofas, home appliances, clothes, lifts, bicycles, and even internet connectivity, solar power, working stations, and money are some examples of peer-to-peer services that can be exchanged or rented out. Combined with technological advances and the hyper-connectivity afforded by the Internet, peer-to-peer service companies are thriving, whether transactions are non-monetary as in trade or barter, or monetary transactions. On this platform of sharing, ownership is taking second seat to access as start-up companies the world over are tapping into the sheer financial profit generated at the crossroads of collaboration, exchange, and the market.

Peer-to-peer service companies offer commodity exchanges between two strangers entering a contract agreement. There is no previous social relationship between giver and receiver, and once the transaction is completed, both parties part ways without strings attached. No other obligations bind them together except for what the implicit exchange contract called for. The networks established through the collaborative economy, in other words connections between people, facilitated through the platform of exchange offered by technology, put a dent in Mauss' division. For one, peer-to-peer sharing engages a higher level of trust between two strangers compared to other commercial transactions. It's one thing for me to go to a store and buy a pint of milk, trusting that the cashier will let me leave with the bottle once I hand over the money; it's another thing entirely to lead a complete stranger to my cow. More than ever before we are making goods and services that are part of our intimate worlds available for consumption by complete strangers. Trust, therefore, has taken center-stage in collaborative economic transactions. Online reviews also play a crucial role in keeping potential clients on track. We are opening our doors and putting up for rent elements of our inner spheres – our couches, our homes, our beds – in ways that have seriously challenged conventional norms of commerce.

These emerging practices of the shared economy, as it is often called, are not as smooth as some enthusiasts would have us believe. This is obvious when looking at the uproar that Uber has created. Taxi drivers are up in arms as the popularity of the transportation service continues to boom, and there are other concerns to be addressed in terms of safety, insurance, legal responsibility in case of accidents, etc as well. While these details are being worked out from location to location, Uber is going strong. But, exactly how "shared" can a service like Uber be on a global scale? I'm more interested in looking at those of us – by and large most of the world – who are at the margins of the shared economy, those on the outside looking in. Renting out your bed, your car, and your home requires that you possess them. Sure, it is much cheaper – not to mention a completely different kind of travel experience – to couch surf in Thailand and meet local Thais your age savvy enough to be connected to the Internet and make use of it for their economic advantage, instead of renting a lonely hotel room or a bed in a hostel. But questioning who gets to participate in this new commodity exchange is enough to realize that the shared economy is not that shared after all. While it works for many, as the growing popularity of the shared services proves, in many other cases it reinforces some of the staggering economic inequalities already in place.

The great thing about peer mentoring is that it does not necessarily require money, since the currency is skill. Another important element for peer mentoring to be put in practice is communication. Communication is the means for making our skills aware to a group of peers so that we can match skill or service offers with skill or service needs. Think of Peer-mentoring as networking taken to a whole new level. Networking in the framework of peer-mentoring is like networking squared, so to speak, because it involves more than accumulating professional contacts: it requires establishing a socially meaningful, reciprocal and interactive system of exchange between two parties who enter a work contract. In many ways, it is our modern version of gift giving, a new twist to the older systems of exchanges that Mauss and Malinowski talk about.

5.

THE SHARING ECONOMY
MAKING A LIVING, ONE GIG AT A TIME

Thinking about Peer Mentoring made me realize how many changes are taking place in our society. These changes are caused partly by current economic and social pressures and partly by the growing awareness that we all have uncultivated resources and unused talents and skills that we could share with others, if we had the opportunity. First, though, we have to do two things: identify specifically what those resources are and find people to share them with. Today's economy seems ripe for this Peer Mentoring model to take hold, as people are now accustomed to the idea of sharing all kinds of resources. Many of us already offer our extra rooms, couches, cars, or office spaces to others for their use. From there, it's not a distant leap to sharing our personal resources with others—our skills, know-how, and contacts—while receiving their resources in return.

The examples I'll use in this chapter are mostly about sharing material resources. This happens within the framework of a large-scale system—a central registry of customers—that manages and facilitates circulation among members. A library is the perfect example. As we'll see later, though, the more personal kind of Peer Mentoring is very different. It consists of directly sharing personal resources with one, (in some cases two) specific colleague—in the context of an agreement, with no money being exchanged. In this situation, no central company or registry is involved. First, let's look at sharing practices that occur in organized and regulated structures like libraries.

Oldies but Goodies: Centralized Exchanges in Action

As soon as I finish writing this section, I'll head across the street to my local library, which offers one of the oldest, most common and trusted forms of 'peer sharing'. This branch also has a small section for recycled (used) books, which have been donated by neighbors and sold as "books for a buck." I booked a private conference room to meet with Gabriella, the anthropologist who wrote the previous chapter. This service, which allows members to use a meeting space, is another shared resource offered by the library. On the way to the library, I'll pass the bike rental stand, which is a citywide bike sharing service. You can pick up a bike at this location, use it for a few hours, and then drop it off at another stand across town.

Other times, I'll pick up a car from the parking lot outside the library, which belongs to a car-sharing service. I just make a reservation online, use the vehicle and a few hours later; I bring the car back to their lot and return to my home. I won't have a bill for parking, insurance, or gas. Now some car-share companies have instituted a new service called "peer sharing." Local car owners can get their vehicles checked out by mechanics, to make sure they're sound, and then offer them to be used by car-share members. The car owner gets paid a rental fee for this and the company can now offer more options to its members.

Today, we are all now part of what is being called 'The Sharing Economy.' This is an intricate network of buyers and sellers or groups of people who partake of a single resource such as the use of compact cars or bicycles in large cities. This has come about with the confluence of two forces. The first is technology: inexpensive computing capabilities now allow a freelance artist to create a company's brochure that can rival the services of a much larger promotion agency at a fraction of the cost. In fact, that freelancer might have been the Art Director of such an agency who was laid off and is working now as an independent contractor. The second force is new social habits. We hear a lot about the "1%," and the growing income disparity in our society. As the gap between the "haves" and the "have-nots" widens, we now have people who have money, but no time, and people who have time but no money.

Getting back to the realm of transportation, there are many variations on the idea of several people sharing a single resource. I recently heard of a young man who had lived in New York all his life, wanted to leave, but didn't know how to drive and had a fear of freeways. He moved to L.A. and now has a car pick him up and take him to his destination by using the app he downloaded onto his smartphone. As a response to raising concerns about the safety of women using ride-hailing apps being driven in cars by men who are not official employees with mandatory ID's, a new niche has been created. It is a variation that started in New York City called She-Taxi which now employs hundreds of female drivers who chauffeur an exclusively female group of customers. As the well-known economist Tom Friedman wrote in the New York Times recently, "the sharing economy is alive and well, and it's thriving in many sectors of the economy and geographic areas."

In addition to personal benefits, it's become terribly hip to be part of the sharing economy. As recently as six or seven years ago, it might have been a source of deep embarrassment and shame for someone of my age and socioeconomic status to be seen driving a ride-share rental vehicle with a prominent logo on both front doors. I would have considered it much higher status to be sporting a BMW or Mercedes, gas-guzzling SUV. Now many feel that it's ecologically tone-deaf to be driving a large vehicle unless it's necessary to transport goods or multiple passengers. Think of your reaction the last time you tried to park next to an oversized SUV. During the same several hours of any day, in any city or town, hundreds of thousands of ordinary people are making use of these shared services. For some, sharing for profit is a natural instinct and is nurtured from an early age.

Zhang Lei, a billionaire investor in internet companies, got his start with a sharing economy when, at age 7, he rented his comic books to commuters waiting for trains at the local commuter station.

In other types of peer sharing, for example TaskRabbit, people who are unemployed or underemployed become "micro-entrepreneurs" by offering skills they have on a network that is organized by areas of skill and geographically. Not long ago, I needed someone to help me organize my thoughts for this book and for some seminars I was planning to give. I went on TaskRabbit and found a work from home mom who had previously worked as an executive assistant, but was now taking on odd jobs, while she stayed home to raise her children. She was located on the other side of the country from me; we discussed the project via email and agreed on a price and due date. She delivered a beautiful job on time. I paid TaskRabbit via PayPal, and it paid her the agreed-upon amount, minus the share TaskRabbit takes.

My niece, who is a busy single rabbi in a small town near Boston, was pregnant and wanted to hire a nanny as soon as the baby was born. She hired a "screener" (who happened to be in Chicago) to interview nannies and gave her a list of the five best candidates in the Boston area. The process took a few weeks; then she interviewed the finalists via Skype and hired one, who worked out wonderfully. She saved herself hours of scrolling through ads and resumes, and since this was her first child, she wanted an expert to help her form a list of criteria and then interview prospects. She paid TaskRabbit for that service. She also wrote a short review of her experience which happens to be a very important aspect of most peer sharing services.

I have used a similar service called fiverr. It is a resource upon which people list gigs they will perform and name a fee (e.g. "I will transcribe your audio for $25"). Members purchase gigs and then communicate with their supplier through fiverr's website. It is quite restrictive, regarding the buyer and seller's direct communication in an effort to prevent people from meeting on the site and then work together outside of the website in an attempt to avoid paying its fees. That aside, I have had some tasks done very well and delivered on time by this service.

Here are some other examples of peer sharing, some of which I've practiced informally for years. When I lived on the Upper East Side of New York City and was working in Northern New Jersey, I purchased a very inexpensive car with a partner, who was a professor at a university in Brooklyn and lived on the Upper West Side. If you know the geography of New York, you'll know how much of a hardship commuting would have been for each of us without a car. Also, the cost of a full-time parking space in either of our neighborhoods would have been prohibitive. So, we shared. He would go to his job, return to Manhattan, and leave me a text message telling me where he had parked the car and when it had to be moved. Parking laws in New York are strictly enforced and you can find your vehicle towed if you overstay your street parking space by even a few minutes. This arrangement lasted for a few years and, in the process, we became great friends. Later, when he and his wife moved to Israel, they even offered me their guest room there for a few weeks.

Professional Sharing

We also see sharing practices in professional services and advice. I belong to a group called SNN, Speaker News Network, a virtual network of about 8,000 professional speakers and trainers. We are sent an e-newsletter every week, as well as several educational offerings in the form of webinars, teleseminars, and advice.

SNN has come up with a wonderful, creative way of attracting a steady stream of good content for the newsletter. We don't pay a membership fee to receive the newsletter. Instead, we are asked to submit two "tips" every quarter to be shared with the entire membership. These can be ideas we have created, better ways to speak and train, websites we've discovered that have helpful information, and even ideas on business travel. This is truly an example of peers helping peers, and, because of the rules, I'm always thinking of ways I can offer a tip or idea to my fellow consultants and speakers.

I previously belonged to a Writers' Support Group in New York City. Rather than being overly easygoing at these meetings and merely talking about writer's block, we followed a strictly disciplined regimen. We met once a week at someone's apartment and we had a group facilitator (a different one each time) who ran the process. Each person was "on" for the whole weekly session; he or she would have prepared a chapter (or a chunk) of work to read to the group and distribute a copy to each member. The facilitator would allow time for the reading, then go around the group to answer questions like: Best line, Worst line, What I learned, What I wish I would have learned, What to edit out, Suggestions for improvement, etc. The person in the hot seat had to just listen; someone took notes of all the comments and ideas for him or her to take home and absorb. Then we'd all have coffee and dessert and a few laughs—and not talk about writing.

We were all writing different genres of work: we had a murder mystery novelist, a poet, a self-help author, a business writer (me), a romance novelist, a screenwriter, a playwright, and even a PR person. But we all got the help we needed, and we were enriched by exposure to other kinds of writing, as well as different perspectives from the other members.

One of the biggest examples of business and professional peer sharing is LinkedIn, which is a vast international network of contacts. As of this writing, there are well over half a billion members in nearly every country, plus thousands of like-minded subgroups, where people can discuss issues of common interest. Unlike Facebook, Twitter, Pinterest, or Instagram, LinkedIn is all about business and professional networking. In my own business, I have found and formed, via LinkedIn, productive mutual relationships with affiliates all over the world. I even visited India recently and was graciously hosted by my affiliate there, who I originally met on LinkedIn. He organized a seminar for 25 of his executive clients; I taught it, and we followed up together for future business. I would never have found this talented professional or benefited from business connections made in New Delhi without LinkedIn.

Another category that is now part of the sharing economy is travel for business or leisure. There are a number of on-line home rental accommodation networks that started when two young Silicon Valley roommates were asked quite unexpectedly to host a few visiting businesspeople from Asia because all the hotels were booked. They had no guest room, so they inflated a few air mattresses and gave their guests a reasonably comfortable (and free) stay. The next time this happened, they didn't refuse their guests' offer to pay. Soon, they were running an ad-hoc bed and breakfast and other friends were renting out their spare rooms, or entire apartments, for short periods. All the guests and hosts were listed on the group's website, which matched up available accommodations with guests who needed them. Payments were made through the site, which deducted a handling fee or commission from the payment amount.

Now this ad hoc startup has become one of the leading on-line home rental accommodations networks is a now a worldwide operation that boasts hundreds of thousands of listings in more than thirty thousand locations. These short-term home rentals provide, an extra income stream for ordinary people to help them pay their rent or mortgage, reasonably priced lodgings for travelers, and a more personal and casual relationship between guest and host. In some cases, guests become hosts when their former hosts visit their town or city. Everything is conducted online providing an abundance of terrific choices in many locations for ordinary travelers. Its quality control system is also online; guests are encouraged to write reviews after their stays. A good review gives a host a few gold stars and of course enhances their reputation. Accordingly, any complaints mar a host's standing. The site publishes them all, without censoring, so customers can judge for themselves.

I once rented out my rent-controlled apartment for short periods while I travelled extensively for business. My landlord found out about it and wasn't happy. I was treading on the thin gray line of legality so I stopped doing it, although the extra money was great. But a rent-controlled apartment is too precious a commodity to risk losing, especially in New York.

There have been disputes between rental and condominium boards with some on-line home rental accommodations networks, with the board claiming that occupants don't have the right to, in effect, operate a bed and breakfast or hospitality service without a proper commercial license.

In the realm of real estate, this time in commercial or office space, small business owners often join up to share a space. When Silicon Valley in California was home to many hundreds of start-ups, some of which couldn't or wouldn't work in people's basements any longer, some smart real estate developers began what were called incubators. A business owner would rent a small space and share common services like secretaries, clerical help, and even photocopy machines and computers. Not only was this a great savings financially for the participants, it also provided an environment for peers to discuss theories, bounce ideas off each other, and share contacts or other resources.

When I started my business in New York City, I fell in love with a 4,000 square foot space in the "Flatiron" district. It was not yet the hip area it is now (some called it Silicon Alley). Still though, the rents were astronomical. With the address being on Madison Avenue I HAD to have it! But there was no way I could afford it on my own. I placed an ad in a few local business magazines and journals and ended up with entrepreneurs sharing my space. We hired a secretary, shared a conference room/library, and helped each other with client problems and business challenges. We became great and trusted friends, often ordered lunch from the deli downstairs and ate together in our conference room, sharing that day's business challenges and triumphs, and, most importantly, offering fresh perspectives to each other. The element of sociability is an important benefit in this arrangement.

Our businesses were vastly different from one another: Michelle ran a small ad agency, Richard helped doctoral students with their research, Albert did corporate and industrial design, I was running a training and consulting business, and Rosemary also did consulting, but it was quite different from mine. What we had in common was a desire to succeed and, a need to reduce overheads. Both issues were solved by sharing a place of business with others. Here we could invite clients (as opposed to working at home in our apartments), enjoy professional companionship, and last but not least, work out of a highly coveted Madison Avenue address. Every year we hosted an "orphans' office Holiday Party" for people who were independent entrepreneurs like ourselves who didn't have an office party to go to. I suppose that this might have been considered to be a forerunner of WeWork.

Now, many companies rent office space to professionals or small business owners. There are companies that rent spaces to attorneys for short and long-term stays called "Suites". They advertise that their offices are "designed by lawyers for lawyers". I'm not sure what actual designers would have to say, but it seems to work very well for their clients. One can rent a conference room for a day to host a meeting or a cubicle for a few months. Others, even just rent desk space, offering short-term rentals—a desk, an office, and a menu of many office services. They are often associated with other "Desk Share" partners around the world. Such firms are capitalizing on several converging trends: increased costs of commercial real estate, which make it prohibitive for many professionals to rent full-time office space; increased travel and business across state lines and internationally, offering professionals "an office in every city"; and the economic benefits of using clerical and other office services on an as-needed basis.

As we can see from all these examples, sharing is definitely the zeitgeist of the moment. As large companies downsize, more and more people are finding themselves (or choosing to be) in the "gig" economy. And while it has worked well for many people, releasing them from the restraints of a 9 to 5 life, there still is a need for human contact, support, and motivation. This is a perfect opportunity for creating a Peer Mentor partnership.

6.

The Peer Mentor Model: A 21st Century version of an age-old practice

We all have an exquisite ledger or balance sheet in which we tally who owes what to whom. We do this every day with countless people in our lives, but not necessarily in ways that are purposeful or conscious. Business is based on a complex arrangement of favors. Yet we do not always make these debits and credits explicit to one another. Therein often lies the disappointment. We have varying expectations (but do not articulate them) and then different levels of fulfillment or lack thereof. The important point is that it is a way to maximize your own resources and use the resources of others all around you. They are available abundantly if you will just look—and ask.

Peer Mentorship, the process (of identifying your strengths and areas of improvement, and then pairing up with another for mutual support) can reduce the feelings of inadequacy and competition we *all* have. Now you can look at someone else's competence as potential help, assistance, and support for you. I also have called this process, "re-source-ing,"

Re-source-ing is when you use your own resources and those of others to achieve leverage and synergy for all to succeed. Peer Mentoring is the method by which you and a partner help each other out in complementary ways. We all have a need to have a champion, a sponsor, a supporter. This is not necessarily in the form of a boss or even a superior but the person will be senior to you (more knowledgeable, more experienced) in a particular skill or resource area. An important difference between Peer Mentoring and other types of support is that this is explicit and specific, rather than random. It is based on complementary skills, resources and needs. This relationship is not necessarily connected to friendship or personal feelings but a business contract, a bargain. While in a sense it is cooler and more distant than friendship, in other ways it's more committed and intimate than other relationships. You are committed to someone else's success as they are to yours, and you are offering your gifts to each other.

At a recent conference "The Organization Woman" I ran the opening session for 150 women using this Peer-Mentor model. The feedback has been overwhelming. When *Working Woman* Magazine ran a one-paragraph description of the workshop, I was flooded with inquiries from readers all over the country asking for more information. My own research with control and experimental groups shows dramatic improvement in goal achievement when individuals use the technique. As a professor of management at Montclair State University in New Jersey, I used the Peer-Mentor pairings as a technique to help the students achieve their learning goals in a specific topic. The students reported that using the process gave them focus and support towards achieving those goals.

I had heard about the exciting work of Barbara Sher, whose books first described the "Women's Success Teams." In this process, aspiring career women formed small teams and assessed what each member had to offer and needed from the other team members. I felt, however, that while I like the principles of the teams, the process would be more focused and specific if it was carried out with just two people. There are many aids and catalysts to success. The Peer-Mentor process is one that I (and by now thousands of others) have found to be most effective. It's a way of combining two very powerful ideas – networking and mentoring – into a daily ongoing support system, whatever business or career you're engaged in.

We all do favors and have implicit bargains with one another. You help me out when I have a problem, and I owe you one. We rarely discuss these hidden contracts with one another, although most people have an exquisitely delicate set of mental balance scales in these matters. Sometimes these balances do not get discussed, and one person feels ripped off, exploited, as if she has been doing most of the giving and not getting enough back. In the most common definitions, a mentor can perform the role of a teacher, a sponsor, a role model, a counselor, or a true believer (later in this chapter, we'll discuss the various definitions of "Mentor" given by Daniel Levinson, noted psychologist). The Peer-Mentor system focuses on many of these ingredients. Yet there is the element of mutual exchange, which is the dominant theme in the system.

The value in these exchanges is that they are not necessarily about friendship, having a great time together, or even about being similar. In fact, the agreement can often work better when there are differences – complementary differences between the people. That is, I am better at A than you are, and you are better at B than I am – I will help you learn A if you help me learn B, and we both wind up with more or better quality than we had when alone. The value at the core of this relationship is that it is slightly more impersonal than friendship but more committed than friendships usually are. That is, the two people have a bargain (a contractual agreement) not to like or love one another, but to support and assist one another in achieving their separate goals. Their common goal is for both people to achieve their separate goals.

There is an objectivity and coolness about this. Less charge is involved than in a friendship, yet it is much warmer than a strictly business relationship. For example, if you ask me, I will give you a critique on how you handled that business telephone call I overheard in a manner that is objective and constructive. The Peer Mentor's purpose is to enhance your style in your business communications so that you are more effective and productive, thereby increasing your chances of achieving the goal you have articulated in your contract with your partner.

Your partner will be attentive to your behaviors that are counter productive, off-purpose, or taking you away from your goal. In this Peer-Mentor contract you have spelled out, your partner's obligation and commitment to you includes telling you how you may be helping or hindering yourself. You establish a relationship with someone who contractually is committed to your success and accomplishment. The agreement or contract you design sets up a way for you to get feedback, support, tutoring, sponsorship, contacts, criticism, or whatever else you may have asked for help with.

Most of us have a great sense of appropriateness in gift giving. The lavishness, the originality, the regularity of gifts we give one another for holidays, birthdays, anniversaries, etc. is a finely entrenched, carefully constructed norm of reciprocity that has usually developed over the years in our relationships. I may usually spend half a day creating and designing a personal collage for your birthday card – making it the most uniquely personal and special kind of gift. If you send me a dollar store item a few times in a row, I may be reluctant to invest my time, love, and creativity in the next card I send to you.

We have all kinds of implicit agreements and act on them every day of our lives. We also exercise balances of reciprocity in business activities. A kind of "you scratch my back, I'll scratch yours" pervades almost every organizational system. In fact, most successful executives cite a network of contacts, personal and business accounts of debts and favors as important keys to their success. The "old boy network ," the informal fraternity in most old line organizations, is a prime example of this. Successful business people have learned these networking skills very early in their careers – how to use other people as resources. Unfortunately, using people often has a pejorative connotation, but people who practice this in the way we are discussing know that there is nothing exploitive intended – they are receiving as much as they're giving.

When I go to Kansas City and need three or four contacts there, I can call one of my contacts who will give me the information I need. I will not need to remind her that when she needed publishing contacts and a place to stay in New York, I came up with both for her. Next time, it will be her turn to ask me for something. These favors won't ever be recorded in an actual ledger, yet we both know what the score is. People who are experienced at this game will be acutely aware when the score needs to be evened up. If the last three times we have had contact, my friend has done something for me, I am likely to go out of my way to think about how I can do something for her. I know that if I do not, the abundant flow of generosity she is sending my way may dry up.

In writing this book, I was active in an interesting exchange of favors. My friend and colleague, an anthropologist, called me for moral support and inspiration for a project that was giving her problems. She had received a grant and a story assignment to go to Tibet (her area of study) to write a story on reciprocity in an agricultural commune. The problem was that she was not able to get a green light from the Chinese agricultural commissioner in Beijing to enter Tibet. A friend of mine, an international businessman from Washington D.C., had recently told me about his forthcoming trip to China and a new trend in international business – barter and countertrade. This is a system of trade in which no money is exchanged, rather, countries make deals to swap goods and services with each other, an update of the old system of barter that has been with us for centuries. I was aware that he had some needs for writing expertise.

I introduced them to each other, and he has since promised to use his influence with the Chinese agricultural commissioner to help her get into Tibet. In exchange for this favor, she has agreed to ghostwrite an article about his international activities in this area. When her own project is completed, she will stay on in China to develop the story about his work. Because I facilitated this meeting, she has agreed to help me with some basic research for the chapter on reciprocity for this book. Doing the research and writing that chapter myself would have taken me weeks, and because I was able to introduce and help two friends, I was able to save myself considerable time and energy. So everybody gets what they need. She gets into China, he gets an article about his business, and I get professional research and advice for my book. Next time around, our needs will stimulate other creative ways we can be of use to each other. It's at times like these, when we are facing unprecedented upheaval, in the business world that we need to find ways to creatively work together and share our strengths with others.

When it came to the final version of this book that you are reading, I teamed up with the very talented and learned Dr. Gabriela Djerrahian, professor of Anthropology at UQAM in Montreal who wrote *Chapter 4: The Gift: Rituals Of Exchange and Contract.*

In another example of this reciprocal system, an acquaintance, a high school English teacher, wanted to learn to parlay her skill of teaching writing into a more lucrative activity. She wanted to teach writing seminars for business people. This is one of the areas I work in as a management consultant. Last week we spent a morning together and I gave her a two-hour briefing on the pros and cons of doing this work as a business by sharing my experiences of successes and failures. In return, she agreed to write and edit some brochures I have been unable to complete for the last several months.

We may run into problems when she starts her business and is a competitor. I have a few choices. On the one hand, I could withhold information from her for fear of the competition possibly stealing potential clients and diminishing a source of livelihood for me. On the other hand, I could tell her everything I know, train her as an apprentice, and develop more of my own business so that as she becomes more experienced, we could be associates and share the client load. My past experience lets me know that once I have become more competent, confident, and successful at something, I felt abundant, generous, and more willing to share. I get a vision of the abundance of clients, business, opportunities, and money out there. When I feel insecure, I feel threatened and see everyone as a threat. By being clear about what I want in return from her, I diminished the threat factor. Consequently, we both increased our competence. Over time we discovered that formalizing these agreements created a unique method for achieving both short-term and long-term goals. The method evolved out of our own needs and has changed greatly based on our shifting interests and concerns.

Some of our method includes the most vital aspects of a mentor relationship.

What is a mentor exactly? Usually she is a person of greater experience and seniority in the world than the protégé with whom she is entering into a partnership. A mentor can be a teacher, a sponsor, a role model, a counselor, or a true believer –someone who's always in your corner, cheering you on. Daniel Levinson, noted psychologist, describes the various functions of these labels:

<u>Teacher</u> – to enhance the skills and intellectual development of the student/protégée

<u>Sponsor</u> – to use her influence in the culture, organization, or milieu into which the protégée needs entry or advancement.

<u>Host or Guide</u> – to welcome the novice into a new social or cultural world, profession, or organization; schooling her in social rituals, initiations, values, customs, cast of characters, politics, or protocols.

<u>Exemplar</u> – to serve as a role model after whom the protégé can model herself.

<u>Counselor or Advisor</u> – to coach the protégé through situations new or stressful; the mentor can give concrete advice and suggestions based on her broader or longer experience.

<u>True Believer</u> – to believe in the protégé's dream, her competence in fulfilling them, and her right to achieve it. In this role, the mentor is an encourager, a cheerer-on, a guide, helping the protégé's sometimes flagging confidence and spirit. This may be the most important mentor role.

Many 'how to succeed' books suggest that we each need a mentor. Although a mentor can be a valuable asset, the suggestion has a number of flaws in its application, namely:

1. There are not enough skilled, successful people higher up in the success ladder who are both willing and able to help each of us.
2. The method keeps people stuck in the 'Pygmalion' or savior fantasy that someone 'up there' will take care of us.

3. There is an imbalance between the receiver and the giver. The mentee is always in a debt or obligation because the mentor is doing all the giving.
4. The process contributes to ignoring the value of people at our own level who have considerable resources to offer.
5. Much of what happens depends on the mentor's personality, her amount of self-esteem. Some mentors are only interested in doing mentoring because of their own narcissism – they need the constant reinforcement of a superior position. Others are very controlling and do not hear or have much empathy for the needs and concerns of the protégé.

There are some concerns that there may actually be an unhealthy emphasis on mentoring these days. One concern is that people will clutch at the idea of getting a mentor just to help them navigate their way up the corporate ladder. Another concern is based on the idea that someone else (a parent, godfather or godmother) can set your life right and help you get what you want. Women, in particular have only recently been able to have female mentors as management levels have become more diverse and balanced between sexes. However, many typically found when looking for a mentor that there weren't as many successful women available who could qualify as mentors. If there were, some often had an "I've made it on my own and struggled through – now it's your turn."

The issue of competition still seems to be quite strong among women, and often a woman who is in a position to groom and mentor a younger, less experienced one may feel threatened as the apprentice becomes as proficient and competent as she is. Women have not been at the upper rungs of organizations long enough to feel automatically comfortable and secure there. The idea of bright, young, assertive women moving in and up can be a disturbing one to some women who feel as though there are only a few spots carved out for women at the top.

Other reasons women are cautious or reluctant to become sponsors or mentors to other women are that they feel as though they must keep their hands – and the record – clean. They may do themselves political and career damage if male colleagues and bosses think they are too prejudiced or aligned with women. Another reason is that mentoring takes time and work, and successful career women often believe they do not have much time to spend on this task. Lastly, some women who have had male mentors believe that younger women would be better off doing the same. Men still have more clout, more power, and more expertise in a majority of areas. Some women, however, like other members of oppressed minorities who have long been tokens and have struggled to get "in," feel a moral obligation to help other women. They may also believe that as more women gain entry and success in the organization, the norms can change to make life easier for the ones who got there first. The competitive attitude, although it still exists, seems to have softened in many circles as evidenced by the women's support networks and groups that proliferate.

In many 'how to succeed' books, both men and women did report, however, that they had a number of helping relationships throughout their careers. These relationships, although not necessarily having the intensity of the mentor relationship described earlier, involved mutual respect and a considerable amount of helping, advising, and counseling. Some mentioned that they identified one person who does a particular thing very well and set out to learn this from her or him. In this situation, they are using the mentor as a tutor – going after a particular skill or expertise that the other person has. What our Peer Mentor system focuses on has many of these ingredients in its form. Yet there is the element of *mutual* exchange, which is the dominant theme in the system.

What are the ingredients in the Peer-Mentor process? You can trade what you do, have, and know.

1. Each person identifies at least one 'resource' – a skill, an expertise, contacts, etc. that she feels she wants from someone else and one resource she is willing to share.
2. The parties make an agreement to use each other's resource to benefit each other.

3. Each commits herself to the other person's achieving her goal and becoming successful, despite the fact that they may experience jealousy, envy, competition, or threat if that does happen.
4. The posture of a Peer Mentor is to keep the other on target, to help push through the fears, blocks, and procrastination, and to believe in the other even when they do not believe in themselves.
5. Each agrees to receive the support, counsel, sponsorship, and advice that is designed in the contract. Each agrees to give what the partner considers a fair trade. The deal may not be in the same currency or area of expertise. Each will try to be explicit and specific in describing clearly what they expect of each other and how they know when they are living up to their ends of the exchange.
6. The feedback they give each other will focus on being objective, specific, and critical of the behaviors or activities that seem counter-productive, not the whole person.
7. The goals and objectives of each partner in the contract are spelled out clearly and explicitly so they each know what the other means. For example, the goal "To get more satisfaction and responsibility from my job" is not explicit or clear enough. How will you know when that's happened? How will your Peer Mentor know that you've accomplished it?
8. They will design strategies, activities, or the vehicle to reach these goals. The goals are the 'what,' the strategies or activities are the 'how.'
9. The Peer Mentor role could take a number of forms. For example, one of the peers may be more politically savvy than the other and might help her peer figure out which projects would get her the most visibility. She may help you score the most political points with your supervisor or other people who have some say over your career and your salary review. Similarly, her peer mentor could help her rehearse the talk she will have when she sits down with her boss.

The Peer Mentor model is based on the idea that pairs have an investment in and commitment to one another. That there will undoubtedly be conflict is seen as a natural and normal corollary of an intimate, committed, and involved relationship. In all our research on human relations, the working through of this kind of conflict or difficulty seems to help strengthen the commitment and interest of the two people, so, in a way, these conflicts are simultaneously positive for the relationship.

This description of the Peer Mentor model may seem a bit complicated, but in practice it is actually pretty simple, as you'll see in the detailed instructions in the next few chapters. I wanted to give you as thorough and detailed a road map as possible, but you may improvise and experiment until you find the process that works for <u>you</u>.

7.

BARTER: HOW MANY COWS FOR THAT SMARTPHONE?

When I began gathering information and my thoughts for writing this book, the idea of barter came to my mind. As we'll see when we explore the main concept of Peer Mentoring, the fundamental exchange that the two people are engaging in is a barter of their separate, not necessarily equal, but equivalent resources, skills, and gifts. Barter, as a form of exchange is not a new concept. In fact, there are numerous historical situations in which it was the method *par excellence*. Much like Peer Mentoring, different yet equivalent goods and services were swapped between two parties. How such goods and services were evaluated and who held the authority to define their value changed over time. In this next section, I introduce a few examples, many of which I draw from the work of historians, where two people or parties entered an exchange contract and engaged in barter.[8]

A BRIEF OVERVIEW OF BARTER

The colonial era in America was primarily a barter economy. Goods included beaver pelts, corn, nails, tobacco, and deerskins. Actually, buckskin trading gave us our modern slang for dollar, "buck." After the American Revolution, the United States began to print paper money, but inflation was so bad that people turned to barter again. It is to be noted that whenever the economy is in poor condition, barter booms. When the Crash of 1929 was followed by the Great

Depression, large numbers of people lost their jobs and cash was scarce as a result. These people still had goods and skills, so they began trading what goods, services, and resources they could offer for food, lodging, or whatever they needed. In 1931, a group of labor activists formed the UCL (Unemployed Citizens League) of Seattle. By 1933, the UCL had created a barter economy for its 200,000 members. Other organizations soon followed, taking the barter concept further. They issued "scrip," substitute money, representing an IOU redeemable at multiple businesses or exchanges. As the economy stabilized, some of the barter organizations faded, but the gas crisis of the 1970's and the recession in the early 1980's led to another rise in barter clubs.

Another dimension also appeared in the form of commercial trade exchanges and brokering business-to-business deals through indirect barter. When international companies use this concept, it is called "countertrade," linking imports and exports in a trade transaction that takes place without money.

BARTER AND EARLY CURRENCIES

Barter is almost as old as civilization. Academics trace its beginnings to around 9000 BC when cattle was first domesticated and considered a tangible asset. People could trade some of their herd (sheep, cows, or camels) for other things, which their family needed: food, water, a spear, or a shield. Believed to be first discovered in Egypt and depicted on the walls of tombs, cowrie shells were used by the Chinese in approximately 1200 BC as a form of currency. By some, they were even considered to hold magic powers. The Chinese were so taken by cowrie shells that they began to copy their shapes in base metals.

In parts of the Middle East, pieces of metal, small enough to carry around, became a more practical currency. Egyptians used lumps of gold in the shape of small sheep because sheep were the basis for their trading. Lydia, a part of what is now Turkey, circulated a bean-shaped coin made of a mix of gold and silver in around 600 BCE. They added a stamped design to their "coins" to attest to their standard weight and value. With that change, lumps of metal no longer had to be weighed to determine their worth. The images of the stamps were of the rulers and of various gods. This form of coin began showing up in Greek, Persian, Macedonian, and Roman empires. Unlike the Chinese coins made from base metals, the new coins were made from scarce, precious metals such as bronze, gold, and silver.

It was the Chinese, in around the ninth century C.E. (the Sung dynasty), who issued the first paper money, at first to offset a shortage of copper. It seemed like a good idea at the time, until the government printed unlimited paper money, causing hyperinflation. By 1455, paper money had become worthless and the new Ming dynasty banned it for hundreds of years. The first bank note in China was not paper, but leather. Historians say that in 1180 BCE bank notes were 1-foot squares of white deerskin, with edges in vivid colors. It wasn't until 1661 CE that the first issue of paper money began in Europe – the Stockholm Bank introduced the first banknotes, but they circulated too many and had to call in the government to help. Sound familiar?

As Europeans came to the Americas, their interactions with Native Americans included barter and direct trades. European traders used beads and trinkets, also a lot of military items like guns and ammunition, and, most importantly, alcohol to trade for territory, food, clothes, and other resources. Native Americans gave strong cultural value and significance to shell beads – the word "wampum," still used as a slang meaning for "money," is a shortened version of the Algonquin word "wampumpeage" or "white shell beads." Wampum carried strong symbolic importance in religious, social, and political practices. Archaeologists have found similar materials and inferred their uses farther south and even on the California coast. When Jacques Cartier first travelled to what is now Canada, he reported that white shell beads were used by the St. Lawrence Iroquois in 1535. He compared those beads to the use of gold and silver as money among the Europeans. By the seventeenth century, wampum became a kind of currency between settlers and Native Americans. The website, nativetech.org quotes a report of the eighteenth century that "a fathom (6 feet) of strung beads of white wampum was worth 10 shillings and double that for purple beads," which shows that English settlers in the colonies used wampum (learned from the people they colonized) as their own coinage.

Over the next several hundred years, barter practices continued in some form or another, particularly during tough economic times, when cash was scarce, but people still needed goods and services.

BARTER IN THE TWENTY-FIRST CENTURY

The 2008 recession has renewed interest in barter, for individuals and for businesses. In direct barter, the biggest challenge was finding someone who wanted what you had and had what you needed. But now the Internet allows you to search the world for the match you want. The "Barter" section on Craigslist exploded in 2008 and 2009 – transactions can be as simple as one family offering school supplies to another family in exchange for home renovations. You can swap houses, vacation condos, cars, laptops, and other devices on many websites like Craigslist. I recently swapped my ancient desktop Mac (from the first line of Macs ever made) for a desk lamp, via Kijiji, a subsidiary of eBay's site in Canada similar to Craigslist (the word "kijiji" means "village" in Swahili). The person who wanted my Mac was a collector of the first line of these fruit colored machines, now considered so clunky and slow. He was missing the turquoise one from his collection. Who would have thought I would find possibly the one person in my town with such a need, and that he would have a desk lamp I wanted?

There are other sites where traders are categorized by location – of course, trades are typically easier when done locally. A variation on straight barter is something called "indirect trade." In this instance, users of a network or system earn credit by selling goods and services for either "community dollars" or "trade dollars," and are then entitled to goods or services (not necessarily similar) but equivalent in value to what they have earned in the network.

USING RESOURCES INSTEAD OF SCARCE CASH: YOU CAN TRADE WHAT YOU DO, HAVE, AND KNOW

One of the most prevalent alternative currencies is Bitcoin, which was one of the first forms of digital currency "cryptocurrency". The system is peer-to-peer; users can transact directly without needing an intermediary. In the barter exchanges described above, the way the money works differs among the different exchanges. In most, members pay a one-time membership fee, plus a monthly administration fee, and then a percentage of each transaction goes to the network. There doesn't seem to be any hard and fast rule about the fees or the commissions – in some networks, the seller is charged a transaction fee; in others, it's the buyer who pays it. Some have given me examples of a split, the commission shared equally between the two members of the transaction. A few businesses I know habitually use barter on a regular basis, without joining a formal barter network. Sometimes, barter is conducted more informally by individuals or businesses that see a one-time opportunity for swapping goods and services with each other.

In my own training and consulting business, I often conduct seminars on Business Communications and Influence in a local hotel. The largest expense involved is the price of the meeting room and the catering for breakfast and lunch breaks. Often, I will contact the General Manager of the hotel and offer several seats to members of their staff (placing a retail dollar value on each seat) in exchange for the room and the food. No money is exchanged, they get a valuable seminar for several of their employees – I get a venue and refreshments. Future possibilities for this relationship: they might invite us to teach the seminar for all of their employees, I might recommend their facility to my corporate or organizational clients.

Additionally, when I was attending Empire State University in New York City, a group of us came up with the vision of a trip to India to study the status of women there. We already had our leaders lined up – the anthropologist, Barbara, and our professor. Barbara's area of specialty was Tibet, and more specifically Tibetan Buddhist nuns. Our professor was an Indian psychologist who had worked for the Fulbright Foundation and had many high level contacts in India in business and government. I wrote a grant proposal to the State of New York, requesting funding for the group trip. I was also asked to be the scribe for the group during the trip. We got the grant. In exchange for my efforts, I got a stipend to defray my expenses. During the trip we met so many influential people that I was able to stay for many months after the group went home to conduct my own research and write articles for local Indian magazines.

Another example of trading my writing or other expertise was when I was finishing graduate school in my new field, Organizational Development (OD). I was an older student and had plenty of catching up to do in the practical application of the theories we were learning at university. I knew I wasn't ready to go out into the world and market myself as a "practitioner." I needed practice. At a conference, I met Neale, a partner in one of the leading OD firms at that time. As we chatted, he revealed that one of the other partners, Peter, was writing a book but needed serious help in streamlining and editing the manuscript. I jumped at the opportunity. In return, they offered to include me in client conferences and give me "floor time" to interact with the client groups and hone my skills. This was a wonderful chance to train from the masters in the field, and I took full advantage of it. I enjoyed editing the book (which indeed needed plenty of editing) and it went on to become a big success. However, I didn't get credit in the "Acknowledgements" section for my contribution. This taught me that, when bartering, one must be very specific regarding what you want and what you are prepared to give.

Right now, I'm writing this chapter from the spacious veranda of my villa at a beautiful hotel in the rain forest in Jamaica. Lucky me! Back home, winter storms rage and temperatures have plummeted. I am the guest of good friends of mine who are developing this property as an eco-resort – they have solicited my advice on how to position and market it to the growing ecology-minded audience. I have traded my consulting services for a stay at this beautiful place, as well as a week at their other boutique hotel in another town.

Several years ago, I was living and working in New York, feeling stressed and burned out. I heard about a fabulous spa, Rancho La Puerta, located just south of San Diego, in Baja California. I approached the Program Directors and proposed that I would conduct a few seminars on Goal Setting and Time Management (very much needed by overly busy and stressed people – their customers). They agreed, and, instead of paying me a fee, we bartered – four days and nights of complimentary stay for me for every two-hour seminar I put on. I did a few sessions and got to stay for over a week. The work was not at all taxing, since these were topics that I taught to executives in my everyday practice back home, although not in leotards and sandals. Some speakers do this with Cruise Ship lines and other vacation destinations. It's nice work, if you can get it, but, of course one must remember, you can't pay your rent with room night credits at exotic resorts.

As we've seen, barter is an age-old practice and continues to this day. We seem to have a natural instinct for "trade". Once we begin the practice, even in small forms, we are likely to become stimulated and more creative in the ways we can swap, exchange, trade our own resources for others which we need.

8.

Peer Mentor: A Unique Partnership Characteristics and Comparisons

The Partnership Characteristics & Comparisons Chart in this chapter enables us to define the Peer-Mentor relationship and to provide an in-depth discussion of that relationship. Each aspect of the relationship is defined (i.e., power, competition, commitment, etc.), and then compared and contrasted with the Peer Mentor elements in each aspect with other known partnerships, i.e. Mentor/Protégée, Friends, Business Partners, Teacher/Student, and parent/child.

The representation I used here is that of the traditional parent-and-child relationship. Parents can and do influence children in many ways, by example, rewards and punishments, moral guidelines, and rules.

I will direct your attention to the chart on the following page as we go through its various elements. In the Peer Mentor relationship, Competition is likely and expected. When that is acknowledged, it is discussed and used to enhance the relationship. In terms of Trust, the goal is to have a high level of trust between the Peer Mentors, as it is the foundation for a strong and productive relationship between the participants. The column of Dependency refers to an interdependent relationship. The Purpose is to assist the growth and development (and advance the goals) of each person in the Peer Mentor relationship. In terms of the Selection Based On, the selection criteria are based on complementary skills, resources, and needs.

Commitment is based on a contract and is always renegotiable. The Balance of Giving–Reciprocity is shared; each offers skills or resources to meet the other's needs. The Currency being exchanged is that of skills, support, resources, and encouragement. Exclusivity does not necessarily apply to Peer Mentors as it does to other partnerships. Depending on their goals, individuals can have many Peer Mentors whose 'haves' and 'needs' are consistent with theirs. What could End or Threaten the Relationship? In the case of the Peer Mentor, the relationship is threatened or may end if either violates the letter or the spirit of the agreement (e.g., breaks confidentiality or works against the peer mentor in some way). However, more positively, the relationship might end if or when both members have achieved their stated goals. By reviewing the chart and the other pair relationships we explore, you will see how they are similar to, or different from, the unique Peer Mentor relationship.

≠	Power	Competition	Trust
PEER/ MENTOR	Shared; each has power in specific area	Expected, discussed, and used to enhance relationship	High
Parent/ Child	Parent has most	Often covert	Varies
Siblings	Unequal	Common, open	Varies
Friends	Shared	Common, often covert	Varies
Spouses	Shared	Frequent, often covert	Implicit; varies
Lovers	Shared	Explicit – low Implicit –high	Varies
Mentor/ Protégé	Unequal	Low	High
Teacher/Student (Coach/Player)	Unequal	Low	Student usually trusts teacher/ coach
Consultant/ Doctor/ Therapist & Clients	Unequal; "professional" has expert power, client has hire/fire power	Low	Varies; should be high for relationship effectiveness
Business Partners	Implicit – equal	Often high and covert	Explicit – high; Implicit – varies

≠	Dependency	Purpose	Selection Based on
PEER/ MENTOR	Interdependent	To help growth and development of each	Different goals; complementary skills, and needs
Parent/ Child	Child depends on parent; later reverse	To raise and develop child	No selection; exc. adoption
Siblings	Mutual; sometimes unequal	Continuation of family relationships	Birth
Friends	Implicit-equal sometimes unequal	Personal support/ Companionship, fulfillment	Similar values, goals, or interests
Spouses	Often unequal	To enhance each other's lives, raise family	Similar or complementary values; attraction
Lovers	Explicit– equal Implicit– unequal	To enhance each other's lives	Shared interests, attraction
Mentor/ Protégé	Protégé dependent on mentor	To "groom" and develop protégé	Protégé's needs Mentor's need to be needed
Teacher/Student (Coach/Player)	Student dependent on teacher/coach	To teach, develop student	Student's need
Consultant/ Doctor/ Therapist & Clients	Client dependent on professional; prof. needs client for livelihood	To "heal," counsel, help, or advise the client	Consultant selected for expertise, empathy, chemistry
Business Partners	Interdependent	Shared purposes & goals; work, productivity and money	Shared goals; complementary skills

≠	Commitment	Balance of Giving and Reciprocity	Currency
PEER/ MENTOR	Contractual; renegotiable	Shared – each gives skills or resources to meet other's needs	Skills, support, resources
Parent/ Child	Permanent, emotional, and financial	Early – parent does most; Later– shared	Love, support loyalty, money
Siblings	Permanent, emotional	Explicit – equal, implicit – often unequal	Love, support
Friends	Long-term, emotional	Explicit – equal, implicit – often unequal	Love, favors
Spouses	Long-term, legal, emotional, and financial	Explicit – equal, implicit – often unequal	Love, support, money, time, sex
Lovers	Emotional, sometimes financial	Each offers different "gifts" to other	Love, support, time, sex, (money?)
Mentor/ Protégé	Implicit, sometimes explicit	Mentor is "giver"	Mentor – experience, skill; Protégé – loyalty, admiration
Teacher/Student (Coach/Player)	Implicit; sometimes explicit	Teacher is "giver"	Teacher – knowledge; Student – loyalty
Consultant/ Doctor/ Therapist & Clients	Long- or short-term contractual	Professional gives expertise; client gives fees	Expertise, money
Business Partners	Contractual; legal, financial	Equal, implicit	Money, skills, loyalty

≠	Exclusivity	Factors that Could End or Threaten Relationships
PEER/ MENTOR	No. An individual can have many peer/mentors	Either violates agreements in contracts
Parent/ Child	Child only 1 set; parents may have many	Death, Divorce
Siblings	In particular sibling relationships	Death, Estrangement
Friends	Not usually	Violation of explicit or implicit pacts
Spouses	Yes – in traditional form	Violation of explicit of implicit pacts, e.g. Adultery
Lovers	Yes – in traditional form	Violation of explicit or implicit norms, pacts
Mentor/ Protégé	Not necessarily	Protégé no longer needs mentor; mentor feels threatened by competition from Protégé
Teacher/Student (Coach/Player)	No	Students completes education; player or coach violates pacts
Consultant/ Doctor/ Therapist & Clients	Not usually, except in conflict of interest	Professional. does not deliver services or violate norms; implicit or explicit agreements
Business Partners	Usually, at least in "primary" business	Violation of explicit or implicit (moral) agreements

As you can see, each type of partnership has many variations to be considered. This is particularly important when it comes to determining the level of commitment a partnership requires, especially that of a Peer Mentor partnership.

9.

GOALS

Until one is committed there is hesitating,
the chance to draw back, always ineffectiveness.

Concerning all acts of initiative (and creation)
there is one elementary truth, the ignorance of which kills
countless ideas and splendid plans:

The moment one definitely
commits oneself, Providence moves too.

All sorts of things occur to help one,
that would never otherwise have occurred.

A whole stream of events issues from the decision,
raising in one's favor all manner of unforeseen incidents
and meetings and material assistance which no man could
have dreamed would have come his way.

—Goethe

ACHIEVING YOUR GOALS

When you set a goal, it thereafter acts like a magnet; you are pulled towards it. The resources you need along the way, which you previously thought were inaccessible, now contribute to your momentum. These resources also are being pulled towards a similar goal. But notice, for a magnet to work best, the object being attracted should not have to take unnecessary detours. Yet, along the way, other magnets may draw the magnet off of its goal-oriented path. This is similar to how goal setting and achieving works for people, too. There are often obstacles, oftentimes, monetary ones, that demand your cooperation on your path to your goals. In fact, the winding road toward your goals may seem, at times, to be headed in the wrong direction. But going with the flow can be an efficient way to reach your goal. The traveler seeking directions may be told by the native, "You can't get there from here;" he doesn't mean you can't reach your goal but that a straight path to that particular goal is not practical. Instead, you may have to backtrack before going forward, or you have to go somewhere else first. But, unless your goal is unrealistic, it CAN be reached.

Goal setting works even better when you have someone to help you, even if it's just cheerleading from the sidelines. Goal setting is where the value of a Peer Mentor can really be of great significance, especially seeing that it works both ways – you get help and support with your goals, as does your Peer Mentor from you. Obviously, when you are working through your goals with your Peer Mentor, they will be focused on helping you achieve your career goals. However, you may wish to create and discuss some of your personal goals as well as they may pertain to your career goals in one way or another.

NO PAIN NO GAIN

When the exercise instructor says "No pain, no gain," they are not saying that pain is the goal, but that there is always some unavoidable price to pay for progress. However, whatever unpleasant side-effects you may have during the process, they need not create a struggle or even slow down your progress. On the contrary, the 'burn' one experiences when exercising, for example, can act as a helpful barometer for judging one's progress. This is likely the time when your Peer Mentor can help you the most.

The fear of discomfort is too easily a rationalization for making no effort at all. Unpleasant side effects distract and discourage a poorly motivated person, but these side effects can actually be turned into opportunities. If you choose to strive to achieve your goals with this attitude, it can take your life from a level which is diffused, like the light from an ordinary electric bulb, to a level which is powerful and concentrated, like that of a laser. Setting goals and objectives are especially important at the start of a trip. Yogi Berra said "When you don't know where you are going, it is hard to tell when you get there." Conversely, when you do know where you're going, getting there is a whole lot easier. A set of objectives creates a clear pathway, which frees you from a whole spectrum of worries and uncertainties.

When you know what you'd like to do or have in the future, you can start preparing logically instead of hoping things will take care of themselves. No one can predict the future, but the better prepared you are for some eventuality, the more confident you'll feel about dealing with whatever life hands you. Learn to recognize that goals and objectives are tools to help you, not trap you. The distinction between goals and objectives is an important one. On the one hand, objectives are a lifetime, ongoing direction. A goal, on the other hand, is a specific, achievable, measurable, event or experience. Setting goals helps you measure progress and focus on the activities you're currently involved in, giving you a feeling of movement. One of your objectives might be to help make life better for those less fortunate than yourself. You may never accomplish the objective completely, but you can set some specific goals and plan specific activities, such as: volunteering to work at the children's hospital, or donating money to your favorite charity.

Many people think of goals in vague terms – they say they want to be happier, have more money, or have more leisure time. A better way to use goals is to make them concrete. Ask yourself, exactly how much money do you want to have, where you want to go on vacation, or when you'll be made department manager. This kind of refining and clarifying takes some effort, but it's worth it. Many people are afraid to set goals and objectives. They're afraid of becoming too tied down or afraid they won't be able to reach the standards they've set, but this need not be a deterrent.

YOU CAN ALWAYS CHANGE YOUR GOALS AND OBJECTIVES

The important thing with setting goals and objectives is to just get started! Successful people achieve so much more because they have a sense of purpose and direction. They are in control of their lives because they set goals and objectives for themselves. If this means altering a goal based on the direction they've started moving, they will do that as well. This allows them to continue moving forward, even if it's in a slightly different direction. People without goals and objectives avoid thinking about the future and procrastinate, drifting without direction. Life is controlling them. The following guidelines should be kept in mind when setting goals and objectives to help you be more successful:

1. Goals Should Be Yours - It's all right to accept advice and suggestions from others, but you will be more motivated to do something if it's something you really want to do.
2. Goals Should Be Written - Keeping goals in your head will not work as effectively as writing them down. Besides being clearer, written goals serve as reminders and records.
3. Goals Should Be Realistic and Attainable – A goal is not a fantasy or a daydream. It should be something you can accomplish with some effort and stretching. Don't set goals too low, but if they're too difficult, you won't believe you can accomplish them and will probably never start. Don't be overly optimistic, either.
4. Goals Should Have Target Dates - Give yourself time limits. Often you will have sub-objectives with their own target dates. If you don't make the target, don't hate yourself – just set a new date.

5. Goals Should Be Compatible - Watch out for conflicts. If conflicts exist, working on one goal may prevent you from achieving another, and then you end up stuck all the way around.
6. Goals Are Not Activities - Once you've set some goals, you'll have to figure out some ways to achieve them. Write down the specific activities you must do to achieve a goal by its target date.
7. Goals Should be Shared - Your Peer Mentor may not have been involved with the creation of your goals and may, or may not be, aware of what you want to accomplish. If you previously created your goals, then by all means share them with your Peer Mentor, no matter where you are along the way in your journey.

As opportunities and obstacles arise, we are often forced to change our goals, but a wise person anticipates the need for change by re-evaluating and renewing goals. You can generate renewed goals periodically in order to stay current with your own internal growth and changes and with the external changes in your work and life. Your goals of a year ago may already be achieved. Or, a major change in your life or career may be the catalyst for you to set new goals. If you've never really thought about goals and objectives, take some time now to do it. Just jot down thoughts as they come into your mind – even if they seem to be just pipe dreams. Write down some goals for the following categories. You don't have to have them in every category, nor do you have to record them in any particular order.

★ Career   ★ Social   ★ Family
★ Personal   ★ Financial

REWARDS

Reward yourself every time you achieve a goal, cut out a time-waster or resist procrastination. If you promise yourself a reward, be sure to give it to yourself. Here are some cheerful suggestions for rewards: sing a song aloud, read a magazine, have a massage, take a lesson in something, jog, go fishing, adopt a plant, take a bubble bath, read your horoscope. Major achievements deserve a special treat.

GOAL SUCCESS MODEL

At one time or another you have had what you considered to be an outstanding success, that is, you achieved some results that you desired which completely satisfied you. This tool is designed to help you identify and repeat the specific strategy that brought you to those positive results. Once you can recognize a personal success model for yourself, you will be able to reproduce the results you want at will again and again!

Step 1: Looking at the Goal

What specific goal do you want to achieve now? Write out specific statements about

- A. How you picture yourself with the goal achieved,
- B. What the physical surroundings will be when that goal is achieved,
- C. What good feelings you will have at that moment, and
- D. The positive things you will say to yourself or hear from others when this goal is achieved

Step 2: Assessing the Motivation to Change

How motivated are you to reach this goal? Circle the letter that most clearly identifies your level of motivation at this time.

- A. It really is only a pipe dream.
- B. I want to reach the goal, but I believe it is unreachable for me.
- C. I think it would be a good idea, but I am uncommitted to it.
- D. I want it, but I'm not sure that this is the right time to go for it.
- E. I want it, and I see that I am not directing my energies toward it.

F. I want to achieve this goal, yet I hold back because I'm not sure of others' reactions to my achievement.

G. I know I want it, yet it is not clear to me how to achieve it.

H. I know this goal achievement will help me to take the next step forward.

I. I want this goal, and I believe others will benefit along with me.

J. Achieving this goal will change my life! I am willing to take the positive steps needed in order to reach it.

Using the letter you just circled, put an **X** next to the corresponding statement and read the explanation.

J - No question! You are clear about wanting the goal and seeing the benefits for all involved.

I, H, G - You are strongly motivated yet not sure about proceeding. Apply the confidence you have in other familiar situations to guide you here. You know that if things don't work out you can always change your plan!

F, E, D - You do want to reach your goal, yet you are putting barriers in the way of your commitment. Imagine putting them aside for now and do the rest of this exercise as if the entire world wants you to succeed!

C, B, A - Your motivation is too low to achieve this goal now. Write out another goal that you truly want to achieve at this time.

Step 3: Looking at the Present State

Where are you now in relation to that goal? Write out specifically how you picture yourself now, what the physical setting you currently see yourself in, why you have not reached that goal yet, and the message you hear from yourself and others because that goal is not yet reached.

Step 4: Support for the Present State

What makes it possible for this present state to exist? Circle those statements that most closely match your own answer to this question.

A. I believe that it always has to be this way.

B. I feel unable to make a change now.
C. I do not see myself doing anything differently.
D. I do not get support from others to go ahead.
E. I tried and could not do anything about it.
F. I am looking too hard for answers in the wrong places.
G. I will not try to change until I know it will work out perfectly.
H. I don't feel right about changing.
I. I should have known how to make this change before now.
J. I tell myself not to try too hard.
K. I feel confused about what is really going on.
L. I feel disinterested in making this happen.
M. I know things could have been better if only I had done something else.

Step 5: Moving to the Desired State

Look at each statement you circled. Now write out the counter-statement to each one, using your own positive statements; write them each 10 times, using an extra sheet of paper if necessary. You may want to use the following, which corresponds to the statements in Step 4 as a guide to forming your own statements.

Examples:
a) I believe that situations can always improve.
b) I feel completely enthusiastic and capable of a change now.
c) I clearly see myself doing many new things.
d) I can always generate support from those important to me to encourage my moving ahead.
e) Whenever I try to, I can improve a situation.
f) I easily find alternatives in the most obvious or surprising places.
g) I can try to change even though I may feel awkward at first.
h) I feel excited about changes.

i) When I look at the past, I see how many times I am grateful for the choices I made.
j) I tell myself that I trust my ability to push forward in the most appropriate ways.
k) I am excited and curious about what is really going on.
l) I think I understand what is going on, and I feel delighted with that knowledge inside of me.
m) I am grateful that I chose the paths I did and know I can make even better decisions now.

Step 6: Reaching the Desired Goal

Based on your statements and work in Step 5, what would you need to happen next to let you know you have reached your goal? What would you have to see yourself doing, and how would the physical surroundings need to be? What feelings will you experience then, as well as what positive messages will you hear from yourself and others important to you? Use your creativity and imagination!

Step 7: Flexibility – the Key to the Goal

Think about how many different ways in the past you have successfully solved problems in order to get what you want. Describe below three or four different approaches you can take to move you toward your current goal. Suppose my goal is ask my boss for and get a raise in salary: I could create a chart or other graphic illustrations to show my boss why the raise I am asking for is appropriate, I could cite several examples of companies where people in positions like mine are all earning more than I am, I could write a chronological history of my achievements for the company, or I could show a spreadsheet of my actions on the job and how much money they have saved for the company.

Example 1:

_____

_____

Example 2:

_____

_____

Example 3:

_____

_____

Step 8: Finding the Key that Fits

As you look back at your responses to Step 7, which one seems most likely to help you achieve your current goal? Here you want to work out a step-by-step plan to reach your current goal. Those successful methods that produced past successes can be applied here. As you work through the steps, however, you will probably find yourself fine-tuning the process you used in the past, adjusting for the new goal, for who you are now, or for the different people and environments you are dealing with this time. But your strategy will most likely be the same or at least very similar.

The First Step Is:

_____

To be accomplished by (Date) _____

The Second Step Is:

_____

To be accomplished by (Date) _____

The Third Step Is:

_____

To be accomplished by (Date) _____

Step 9: Success!

At this step you will want to review all the previous steps and transfer to your calendar the dates you indicated in Step 8. Achieving a goal takes planning a strategy and being able to visualize the outcome you want. It takes being able to shift gears and plans if the approach you are using is not working well. Keep in mind that if you don't know what the guideposts are along the way, you will never know if you are moving in the right direction! Repeat these steps for continued success!

GOAL SETTING EXERCISE

Here is an exercise that will help you formulate a well-stated goal. Some of the following goal statements are stated correctly according to our guidelines, and some are not. Write your reaction to each statement. Write in the changes you feel are necessary then read our commentary on each that follows.

1. To give up smoking.
2. To lose weight by July 15.
3. To read one novel a month for the next twelve months, spending no more than five hours a week, at a cost not to exceed $100.

Commentary:

1. To give up smoking - Obviously, you will need, at the very least, a target date. It would be better to say, "To give up smoking by January 16." If you need to involve products or programs that incur some expenses, you could say, for example, "To give up smoking by January 16, and spend the $200 workshop fee necessary to do so."

2. To lose weight by July 15. You must identify how much weight you want to lose. It would be better to say "To lose 5 pounds by February 7." As with the smoking example, include cost factors if necessary.

3. To read one novel a month, spending no more than five hours a week, for the next twelve months, at a cost not to exceed $200 – This goal as stated is acceptable; however, listing which novels you plan to read might be typical of the kind of detailed planning we discuss next.

SETTING PRIORITIES

Setting priorities simply means deciding the order in which you want to accomplish certain tasks. You set priorities everyday of your life. What you do is determine that it is more practical to make a grocery list before going to the supermarket or realize that it makes more sense to take a course in accounting, so you can be prepared for – or attract – a promotion. Look over your list of goals and decide which items are of the highest priority for you. Pick the two goals in this top category and put an "A" next to them. Pick the next two most important items and label them "B." Now pick those goals that will be in your "C" category, those that are goals, but are the least important to you at this time. You can, of course, break them down further: A-1, A-2, B-1, B-2, and so forth. Use this list to set goals for five years, one year, and six months. The chart on the next page will help you set objectives for all areas of your life.

Remember, goals must be specific, concrete, and measure-able. Yes, this is work, but to get what you want from life, you must first know specifically what that is and what to do to get it. This exercise will help you find out what is important to you. Setting goals gets easier with practice. Like most things, the first time is the hardest. The good news is that most people who do it swear that there is something magical about it. Just writing down goals has something to do with making them happen. Your desires and dreams are valuable, and they could be realized – but not if they remain top secret, perhaps even to yourself. As you can see in the below chart, each category applies to an area of your life. As specifically as you can, write down what you would like to be, do, or have for each category.

	5 YEARS	1 YEAR	6 MONTHS
Money			
Career			
Income			
Intimate Relationships			
Friends			
Family			
Residence			
Transportation			
Travel			
Material Possessions			
Recreation			
Health			
Spiritual			
Education			

1. **Money** - How much would you like to be earning in five years? How much money would you like to have saved? Be specific – write the dollar amount.
2. **Career** - What title, job function, or responsibilities would you like to have?
3. **Intimate relationships** - Would you like to be married? Single? Have children?
4. **Social relationships** - Would you like to have more friends? End some relationships? Change the quality of some friendships?
5. **Family relationships** - Would you like to improve communication with your mother? Have clearer understandings with your children?
6. **Residence** - Would you like to buy a house? Sell the one you have? Live in the country? Redecorate?
7. **Transportation** - Would you like a new car in five years? What kind? What color? Get rid of a car and join a car-sharing service?
8. **Travel** - Where would you like to visit? For how long? With whom?
9. **Material possessions** - What would you like to acquire in five years? A new smartphone? New furniture? Designer clothes? What would you like to get rid of?
10. **Recreation** - What activities would you like to have as regular fun in your life? Go to the theatre? How often?
11. **Body Health** - Would you like to lose fifteen pounds? Jog three times a week? Get regular dental checkups?
12. **Spiritual** - What spiritual practice goals do you have? Meditate every day? Be mindful during meals?
13. **Education** - Would you like to go back to school? Take a drawing or painting class? Learn to play the guitar?

CREATIVE TENSION

Given your present life and circumstances, goals should be realistic and attainable, as we've stated before. Objectives might be lofty, or sound unrealistic. After you've had some practice with setting and achieving goals, you may find that you will be more confident and want to set higher ones. This adaptability will give you the capability of living with a moderate degree of uncertainty and anxiety (this is called "creative tension"). Success-driven people push up toward their goal, rather than lower their goal to a level that is easier to reach. Rather than make the required effort to reach the higher goals, less motivated people settle for more reachable substitute goals. This is entirely up to you. Remember, these are your personal goals, and you can always change and adjust them as you go along. Once you have thought about, set, and written down goals, you may find interesting opportunities in your path.

When it comes to achieving the goals you have set, your Peer Mentor's help will be invaluable. Think of the times when you were driving in a new place by yourself and had no one there beside you to help navigate you to your destination. Just think how much easier it is when you have someone there to help you navigate, even when using GPS. I think this bears repeating, Goethe said:

The moment one definitely commits oneself, Providence moves too. All sorts of things occur to help one, that would never otherwise have occurred. A whole stream of events issues from the decision, raising in one's favor all manner of unforeseen incidents and meetings and material assistance which no man could have dreamed would have come his way.

10.

Skills Inventory

As mentioned in earlier chapters, now that you have set your goals, please choose ONE that is most important to you, using the "how will I know when I'm there" question, so that your Goal achievement will be measureable.

Now identify what skills, resources, and talents you already have to assist you in achieving your goals. Then you can use this list to identify the skills and resources you still need to achieve the goal. This will help you in searching for a Peer Mentor, since you will have a clearer idea of what you need help with, and what you are confident about offering. You will have a clearer idea of what criteria you will use before you even approach someone to be your Peer Mentor.

The following is a list of "gifts" you possess, indeed in such abundance that you are willing to offer them to your Peer Mentor; likewise, they will also have skills, resources, or abilities to offer you. This list is by no means complete; it is only meant as a starting point to get you thinking about your own specific resources. Some of these items may trigger your thoughts that will help you create your own lists. All of these can be useful to put in writing on your actual Agreement and in cases where the skill or resource sounds very general, you can break it down into measurable components. For example, suppose one of the skills you have to offer is "writing skills." How can you offer those in a way that is measurable to help your partner? Well, you might ask them what the best way you can help is. They might request that you show a sample of a job application letter as a template they can follow. This is a way to make a specific request and offer from a wider skill set.

You can now begin to stockpile the list of skills you bring to the table. Feel free to make notes right on the page, and soon, you'll have your very own personal inventory list of skills, resources, and "gifts."

MY TRANSFERABLE SKILLS

I can:
- ☐ Meet deadlines
- ☐ Supervise others
- ☐ Increase sales or efficiency
- ☐ Accept responsibility
- ☐ Instruct others
- ☐ Solve problems
- ☐ Manage money/budgets
- ☐ Manage people
- ☐ Meet the public
- ☐ Organize people
- ☐ Organize/manage projects
- ☐ Research – topic(s) from library/internet sources; interviewing people; finding knowledgeable contacts
- ☐ Manage my time

I have a(n):
- ☐ Ability to delegate
- ☐ Ability to plan
- ☐ Desire to learn & improve
- ☐ Good time management
- ☐ Computer skills
- ☐ Mathematical knowledge and skills
- ☐ Technical Expertise – understanding, interpreting technical manuals, descriptions, re-writing into lay language.

☐ Written communications skills

I am:

☐ Results-oriented
☐ Customer Service-oriented
☐ A team player

OTHER TRANSFERABLE SKILLS (DEALING WITH THINGS)

I can:

☐ Use my hands
☐ Assemble or make things
☐ Build, observe, inspect things
☐ Construct or repair
☐ Follow instructions
☐ Operate tools and machinery
☐ Drive or operate vehicles
☐ Repair things
☐ Use complex equipment
☐ Repair mechanical devices, equipment, furniture, electrical, or plumbing
☐ Design information processes, educational seminars/classes, advertising and PR campaigns

I have:

☐ Communication skills
☐ Customer Service skills
☐ Computer skills - programing, operating systems, software proficiency and data analysis
☐ Problem-solving skills
☐ Project management skills

I am:
- ☐ Safety conscious
- ☐ Good at troubleshooting – finding sources of problems (in mechanical systems, in human interactions)
- ☐ Good with food – cooking, serving, presenting, or giving nutritional information about it

DEALING WITH DATA

I can:
- ☐ Analyze data or facts
- ☐ Investigate
- ☐ Audit records
- ☐ Keep financial records
- ☐ Balance money
- ☐ Calculate, compute
- ☐ Classify data
- ☐ Compare, inspect, or record facts
- ☐ Count, observe, compile
- ☐ Research
- ☐ Handle detailed work – organizing papers, receipts, inventory
- ☐ Develop budgets, create financial systems, maintain records of expenses, payments, or sales

WORKING WITH PEOPLE

I can:
- ☐ Care for
- ☐ Confront others
- ☐ Counsel people
- ☐ Demonstrate something
- ☐ Supervise
- ☐ Speak in public
- ☐ Help others
- ☐ Teach
- ☐ Interview others
- ☐ Anticipate needs
- ☐ Take orders
- ☐ Listen
- ☐ Serve
- ☐ Work with others
- ☐ Negotiate
- ☐ Understand

I am:
- ☐ Patient
- ☐ Persuasive
- ☐ Pleasant
- ☐ Sensitive
- ☐ Supportive
- ☐ Diplomatic
- ☐ Tactful
- ☐ Insightful
- ☐ High energy
- ☐ Open-minded

- ☐ Kind
- ☐ Adaptable
- ☐ Outgoing
- ☐ Sensitive to foreign cultures – cultural customs and traditions, languages, cuisine, lodging, and shopping

USING WORDS, IDEAS

I can:
- ☐ Articulate
- ☐ Innovative
- ☐ Communicate verbally
- ☐ Be logical
- ☐ Remember information
- ☐ Research
- ☐ Create new ideas
- ☐ Design
- ☐ Speak in public
- ☐ Edit
- ☐ Write clearly
- ☐ Understand the big picture
- ☐ Persuade others to see another point of view
- ☐ Create marketing and promotion strategies
- ☐ Work on details
- ☐ Generate support for ideas
- ☐ Listen to, understand, analyze, summarize contents of speech, conversations, interviews, or presentations
- ☐ Write proficiently – copyrighting for sales, speechwriting, presentation writing, editing, or technical writing
- ☐ Interview effectively – job applicants, guests on talk shows
- ☐ Speak, write, and interpret more than one language

LEADERSHIP

I can:

- ☐ Arrange social functions
- ☐ Motivate people
- ☐ Negotiate agreements
- ☐ Plan
- ☐ Delegate
- ☐ Run meetings
- ☐ Direct others
- ☐ Explain things to others
- ☐ Get results
- ☐ Share leadership
- ☐ Think of others
- ☐ Direct projects
- ☐ Solve problems
- ☐ Take risks
- ☐ Empower others
- ☐ Provide nutritional advice
- ☐ Sell
- ☐ Negotiate
- ☐ Influence others to see your point of view
- ☐ Coach – individuals or teams in athletics/fitness; individuals or groups on speeches, media appearances, or court appearances
- ☐ Advise – giving financial counsel or personal advice
- ☐ Counsel – personal/family issues; helping people with personal/career concerns, or educational plans
- ☐ Plan - organization strategies, marketing strategies, fund-raising events, or social events

I am:
- ☐ Decisive
- ☐ Self-motivated
- ☐ A team builder

CREATIVE, ARTISTIC

I can:
- ☐ Dance
- ☐ Perform, act
- ☐ Draw, sketch, or render
- ☐ Present artistic ideas
- ☐ Play instruments
- ☐ Garden
- ☐ Cook, serve, present
- ☐ Organize – ideas, closets, papers, or writing
- ☐ Promote – through social media or one-on-one.
- ☐ Display effectively – ideas in artistic form; pictures for display, photos, art, or visuals for presentation.
- ☐ Style – homes, rooms, or fashion

I am:
- ☐ Artistic
- ☐ Expressive

OTHER

I have:

- ☐ Contacts – in a particular field, industry, organization, city, country
- ☐ Unused Resource – empty apartment, home, office, car truck RV, boat

I know about:

- ☐ Medicine
- ☐ the Law
- ☐ Politics
- ☐ History
- ☐ Economics
- ☐ Travel
- ☐ Foreign Cultures and Customs
- ☐ Foreign Languages
- ☐ add your own areas of knowledge and expertise here

ADD ANY OTHER TRANSFERABLE SKILLS THAT YOU THINK YOU HAVE:

- ☐ _____
- ☐ _____
- ☐ _____
- ☐ _____
- ☐ _____
- ☐ _____

After going through all these skills and resources, you probably have a much larger list than you did before. Highlight the ones that are particularly strong for you and add some notes to describe the specifics of that skill and how you might offer a measurable portion of it to your Peer Mentor. Ask her to do the same. Having assessed and further developed your skills inventory, you will both be well-prepared to work on your Peer Mentor contract and have a wide variety of resources and "gifts" to offer each other towards achieving your separate goals.

11.

How and Where to Find a Peer Mentor

Once you have set a clear a measurable goal, identified the skills/resources you have towards achieving it, and what you'll need help with, now you are ready to seek a Peer Mentor.

Where and how will you find one? Well, once you begin looking, you'll find potential "Success Buddies" are all around you! Here is a list of some places where you might find a good Peer Mentor.

1. At your regular job - There may be people around who have different job descriptions or functions, but you may like them and find they have skills that you would like to learn. Be sure not to overlook those in different parts of your organization simply through the everyday workings of your job. Or you might meet people in Inter-department teams or task forces. You might even meet someone at the company's softball team (we will get to non-business activities in just a moment). At these kinds of meetings, you'll have plenty of opportunity to see people's skills and character in action (as well as their deficiencies or flaws). If you do see someone who looks promising you can invite her or him for a meal or coffee to talk about it further. What do you have to lose? If they're not interested in forming a Peer-Mentor relationship with you, you might still make a new friend.

2. In training or professional development meetings - In this kind of setting, you may be meeting people from different organizations or companies, different departments or areas of your own organization, or even countries or states far from your own. You are all learning together, so it's a great way to observe how someone interacts with the instructor, with other students, and what skills or bright spots they exhibit. Again, you can take the initiative to ask the person to sit down with you sometime during the event to discuss this new educational tool you have discovered.

3. Work travel - This could be one of the best opportunities of all – if you go to a conference, there may indeed be some of your colleagues attending, but there will likely be hundreds, maybe even thousands, of other interesting people you don't know. Of course, you may only get to meet a fraction of them, and you'll be able to practice the skill of approaching strangers at pretty low risk because if it doesn't go the way you'd like it to, you'll probably never see them again.

4. Extra-curricular activities - You may find people in settings other than the work or professional spheres. For example, you might meet someone at your place of worship, fundraisers, charitable activities, or informal receptions, All of these give you a chance to observe other people on their 'off' time. You may observe how they interact on a volunteer project team, how they behave one-on-one. Do you participate in team sports, play bridge or Scrabble regularly with the same people, belong to a choir or other musical group, go to a book club, or participate in a trivia group? All of these may present great opportunities to see people in a different light, get to know them, assess their suitability as a Peer Mentor, and approach them with the idea. If they're not interested, nothing is lost. And the best thing about finding a Peer Mentor in these situations is that you already have a common interest – beyond that, the success of your Peer Mentor partnership will lie in your shared commitment, ability to focus on your goals, and willingness to support each other.

5. The online world - These days, we don't even have to leave the house to find tens, hundreds, or even thousands of contacts, friends, or connections to consider as Peer Mentors. Of course, as with all relationships, you must take the time to get to know, like, and trust the one or more people you may have identified as potential Peer Mentors. For example, you may begin as members of the same professional group on LinkedIn, and then move to emailing each other directly. Next, you might arrange for an initial Skype call, then step up the frequency to weekly or bi-weekly Skype calls, and then possibly come up with a project to work on together.

I met Sandy Chernoff online, a consultant and trainer in Vancouver. We connected via LinkedIn, started emailing each other, and then proceeded to a bi-weekly standing Skype appointment. We were both working on writing projects and provided a progress report to each other during those calls. The content of our projects wasn't really important – it was the process that counted. After several conversations, I learned that she was working on an e-learning curriculum, and she learned that I was writing this book. During one call, I committed to finishing two chapters, and she promised to finish three modules of one of her e-courses. We were in a Peer Mentoring relationship, even though we hadn't filled out the 'paperwork' (the Peer Mentor Agreement).

During the course of our discussions, she introduced me to Dennis, in Athens, Greece, whose business specialty is LinkedIn Profile makeovers for members. I was interested in perhaps using his services to improve my profile. In the meantime, though, he and I talked via Skype several times and came up with the idea of writing an article together, using a combination of our expertise. It's called "How to Create Influence on LinkedIn; Keywords and Beyond."[9] We posted the link to my LinkedIn connections as well as to his. It's been posted on LinkedIn Pulse and has generated a lot of buzz for us both.

He has helped me re-design my LinkedIn Profile, and how to craft successful invitations. I also learned how to do targeted searches. I started with nearly 6,000 connections, and because of these efforts, I now have close to 15,000. His business has become so successful that he is now regularly, being asked to do public speaking (like one he did recently at the Mayor's office in Athens). I coached him about public speaking, sharing what I know about preparation, engaging an audience, etc. So far, our reciprocal relationship has been quite informal.

This process has been very informative because we have gotten to know each other better. I learned that he is absolutely always prompt for our calls, takes the initiative in our shared writing tasks, is fair – in fact, generous – about taking credit, and keeps his commitments. These are all qualities I value in a Peer Mentor, so I believe we have a great start.

As in setting goals, once you have in your mind the idea of finding a Peer Mentor, you might see people you meet, or people you already know, in a different light, viewed through the prism of "is this a possible Peer Mentor for me?" You may find yourself more open to the process and perhaps begin a conversation with a likely Peer Mentor. Who knows where it could take you?

12.

THE AGREEMENT

To help you achieve your goal, you need a fellow dreamer, a Peer Mentor to work with you. This Peer Mentor can be a friend, a co-worker, some other close associate, or a complete stranger. Typically, it is better if your Peer Mentor is not your spouse or best friend. Your Peer Mentor need not be a professional (such as a member of clergy, social worker, or counselor) but should be a person who has resources or skills which you do not and who has agreed to support you by sharing their knowledge and skills with you. This is the person with whom you will review your objectives each week, making sure your goals are specific and checking to see if you are sticking to your objectives and eliminating any activities that waste time or energy. In turn, you agree to offer her your support, resources, and skills. I also call this process "re-source-ing" as it is a method for you to use the resources of another person in order to help you achieve your goals.

The agreement on the next page is designed for you and your Peer Mentor to organize and formalize your mutual support. This is not a legal document of course, but in many ways, it can feel more binding than an actual one, because of your motivation and commitment. In order to start your Peer Mentor relationship off on the right foot, you should:

1. Make copies of the contract so you leave the original blank.
2. Identify one goal (on the left).
3. Write (on the right side) the indicators or measures that will tell you when you have reached your goal.
4. Indicate the resources required in order to achieve your goal.
5. In the "Strategies" section, describe first what you will do for yourself in order to achieve your goal and then what your Peer Mentor will do to support you. Some important ways are

indicated (listening, advising), and you can find lists of skills and resources in the previous Chapter.

6. You can give a personal example of how you intend to use each one to support your partner. Photocopy the page and give a copy to your Peer Mentor.
7. Sign each contract. The signing can be the occasion for some personal ceremony (such as during lunch at a special place) that can be repeated when the goals are reached.
8. Agree on specific times to review and renew your contract with your Peer Mentor.

Although you may have many goals you want to work toward, it is important that you choose ONE to begin working on with your partner. It is a new process and having the focus, for each of you, on just ONE of the goals will ensure a successful outcome more quickly. Then, you can both build on that success by choosing another goal to accomplish.

PEER MENTOR CONTRACT

Goal – Desired Outcomes   **Indicators/Measures**

_____   _____

_____   _____

_____   _____

Resources Required   **PEER MENTOR will support me**

_____   _____

_____   _____

_____   _____

Strategies:

I will _____ for my Peer Mentor:

❏ Listen   ❏ Teach
❏ Advise   ❏ Connect
❏ Share Skills   ❏ Other

_____
_____
_____

Signed _____ Dated _____
Signed _____ Dated _____

13.

COMMUNICATION SKILLS FOR SUCCESS WITH YOUR PEER MENTOR CONTRACT

Once you create your contract with your Peer Mentor and begin meeting – either in person, via videoconference, by email, or on the telephone – there are certain guidelines for the process of communication. The 'what' part of your communication is the content of how you and your Peer Mentor are each progressing towards your goals and the actual sharing of resources with each other. The 'how' of your interactions is the process, the manner in which you communicate various aspects of your ongoing relationship. For example, you may be frustrated with the number of times your partner cancels or shows up late to these meetings. Or, you may feel that the amount of time you have devoted to their goal or achievement far exceeds the amount of help you have received. Your Peer Mentor may feel the same way in these, or other, aspects of your relationship. Like any good partnership, relationship, friendship, or business alliance, all will not go smoothly nor will they be equal, or fair, all the time. It is important to have a skillful and tactful way to express your feelings and describe your expectations to be able to tell your Peer Mentor what you are pleased about and where you feel things are falling short.

FEEDBACK GUIDELINES

Providing feedback is one way of helping a person change or alter one of their behaviors. It is a way of communicating to a person (or a group) that gives the person information about how something affects others negatively. Feedback helps an individual keep their behavior on target and thus better able to achieve their goals. Here are some criteria for useful feedback:

1. It is descriptive rather than evaluative. Describing your own reaction allows the person to use the feedback as she sees fit. Avoiding evaluative language reduces the need for the person to react defensively.

Here's an example of evaluative language that should be avoided.

> *"Rodito, your presentation was disjointed."*

Here's an example of evaluative language that you should use instead.

> *"Rodito, I found it challenging to follow your trend of thought." (Using "I" language).*

2. It is specific rather than general. Telling a person that they are domineering will not be as useful as telling them that they did not listen to what others said in the most recent meeting, and so others felt forced to either accept their arguments or face attack from them.

Here's an example of language that you should avoid.

> *"Thalia, the way you handled yourself in the meeting was unprofessional."*

Here's an example of language that you should use instead.

> *"Thalia, I noticed that you interrupted, Mai and Irene during the meeting. It would be best if you waited until they finished what they had to say.*

3. It takes into account the needs of both the receiver and the giver of feedback. Feedback can be damaging when it only serves one person's needs and fails to consider the needs of the person on the other end.
4. It is directed toward behavior the receiver can do something about. Frustration only increases when a person is reminded of a shortcoming over which they have no control.

5. It is solicited rather than imposed. Feedback is most useful when the receiver formulates the kind of question those observing them can answer.
6. It is well timed. In general, feedback is most useful when given at the earliest opportunity after the behavior has occurred depending, of course, on the person's readiness to hear it and the support available from others, etc.
7. It is checked to ensure clear communication. One way of doing this is to have the receiver try to repeat and rephrase the feedback she has received to see if it corresponds to what the sender had in mind.

Feedback is a way of giving help; it is a corrective mechanism for the individual who wants to learn how well her behavior matches her intentions.

HOW TO RECEIVE CRITICISM

Many of us are uncomfortable with criticism. Receiving criticism may make you feel hurt or put down; however, unless you clear up assumptions about others and state what your own needs are, you will repeat unhelpful, and possibly damage patterns. Although it's hard to receive, you must remember that criticism can help you in the future. The best way to effectively receive criticism is to really listen to the person assessing you, and to give an assertive response back, if necessary. An assertive response to criticism consists of asking for clarification in a firm, calm and direct manner while indicating if you consider the criticism unfair. For example, if your boss says, "This report is inadequate, do it over," your assertive response might be, "I worked hard on this report and think I did a good job. Please explain to me what, specifically, about the report you consider inadequate."

HOW TO GIVE CRITICISM

Giving criticism involves providing negative feedback on someone's work, personal actions, or habits. Criticism, given unassertively or without compassion, may lead you to believe that you have hurt someone's feelings or worry she won't like you. Not giving criticism at all may leave you feeling frustrated, hurt, puzzled, or dissatisfied. In order to give criticism effectively so as not to offend the person you're criticizing and have them hear your complaint and want to change for the future, try to follow these guidelines:

1. Provide criticism assertively by being direct and specific. Indicate what the problem is as a statement rather than as a question. For example: "Please do your share of the paperwork. I feel uncomfortable that you leave that part of your daily work so often. I need those figures for my work on a regular basis."
2. Provide the criticism as soon as possible after the incident. For example: "I want to speak to you about something that bothered me at the meeting this morning. Can we meet for lunch today?"
3. Make sure your criticism refers to the specific problem rather than the entire person. For example: "I feel angry and upset when you use my ideas at meetings without giving me credit."
4. Try to formulate your criticism in a positive way. For example: "Points x and y should also be included in this report, but otherwise it is very good. I can tell you put a lot of work into this."

Once you get into the rhythm of communication with your Peer Mentor, your relationship should run smoothly and your progress towards your goals will be accelerated.

14.

PEER MENTOR PROGRESS ASSESSMENT

At this point you have now identified the goals you want to work on, have chosen a Peer Mentor, discussed, and negotiated how you will help each other. After a few weeks, you may want to use these questions and share them with your Peer Mentor, as well to see how the relationship is going.

As you review these questions, other issues may come to your mind. Feel free to add them to the list.

The Goal I am working on is:

_____
_____

2. This is the first time I have written down my Goals   **yes**   **no**

3. The Skill/Resource I am offering my Peer Mentor is:

_____
_____

4. I am helping my Peer Mentor by:
_____ reviewing their goals
_____ providing them with resources (books, websites, contacts)
_____ teaching them this skill
_____ practicing the new skill
_____ providing feedback

5. My Peer Mentor is offering me Skill/Resource:
_____
_____

6. My Peer Mentor is helping me by:
_____ reviewing my goals
_____ providing me with resources (books, websites, contacts)
_____ teaching me this skill
_____coaching me in this skill
_____ practicing the new skill
_____ providing feedback

7. Our agreed upon method of keeping in touch is:
_____ phone calls
_____ video calls (WhatsApp, Zoom, Skype)
_____ in-person meetings
_____ email

8. Methods we are using
_____ listening
_____ counseling
_____ advice-giving
_____ teaching a skill
_____ role-playing

9. I am finding this process
a – distracting me from other things
b – time consuming
c – somewhat helpful
d – moderately helpful
e – very helpful, changing how I do things

10. The process is
_____ anxiety-producing
_____ fun
_____ one that I can use with other goals
_____ interesting – a learning experience
_____ other (please specify)

11. My partner
_____ understands me
_____ listens well
_____ offers good suggestions
_____ doesn't really understand me
_____ isn't very helpful

12. What I have noticed about myself is:
_____
_____

13. What I have accomplished towards achieving my goal is:
_____
_____

14. I think this process is:
_____
_____

15. Please check off all the words that you feel best describe you (and ones you have learned about yourself since beginning this process)

- ❏ intuitive
- ❏ stubborn conventional
- ❏ good at detail
- ❏ resourceful
- ❏ rational
- ❏ fun-loving
- ❏ creative
- ❏ obliging
- ❏ curious
- ❏ contented
- ❏ flexible
- ❏ analytical
- ❏ enterprising
- ❏ reserved
- ❏ independent
- ❏ serious
- ❏ methodical
- ❏ dominant
- ❏ cautious
- ❏ relaxed
- ❏ impulsive
- ❏ original
- ❏ demanding
- ❏ big picture thinker

What I have learned in general since beginning this process:

_____
_____
_____
_____
_____
_____
_____

Conclusion: The Beginning

Now we are at the end of the book, but hopefully, at the beginning of **your** successful Peer Mentoring journey.

I started this book with a simple goal: to create a detailed "how-to" about Peer Mentoring and give readers a step-by-step process to help get support for and achieve their goals.

As I got further into the study and the process of Peer Mentoring, I looked into some of the historical and anthropological foundations of barter and reciprocity, gift-giving and exchanges. And of course, the sharing economy" is all around us – we're either participating in resources like Uber, Airbnb, Fiverr and so many others, or learning about them via Twitter, online news sites and other sources.

I found all of this information fascinating, and decided to include it. I hope you found it interesting as well, seeing as how it connects ancient practices with the new application of Peer Mentoring.

You may have found your Peer Mentor and have already started working on your goals. Maybe you have even initiated the Agreement process with them.

I hope you are as excited as I am about this process, and the great catalyst that it can be, to move you towards accomplishing all you desire in your personal life and especially in your career.

I would love to know how you are doing. How is your trip along this path going? What are the successes, the challenges, and the bumps in the road? Perhaps you and your Peer Mentor have decided to improvise, to do a different version of the Agreement or the process. I would love to hear about your unique twists and tweaks.

You can write to me at **ez4u@ezinfluence.com** or visit **www.ezinfluence.com** to view our other books, products and services.

Whatever your goals are and however you are using your Peer Mentor to achieve them, I wish you the greatest success in all aspects of your life!

Also by Elaina Zuker

INFLUENCE:
The 7 BIG Secrets in 7 Little Minutes

Influence. Everyone Wants It. How To Get It?

Success in today's business world is not dependent just on knowledge which can quickly become outdated or contacts who vanish overnight but an inner resource—the ability to influence. In this highly practical guide, communications expert Elaina Zuker outlines how this essential portable power can be learned, practiced, and mastered to serve whenever and wherever we are.

Influencing is one of the critical business skills required for success today. Strong interpersonal and influencing skills are essential as we work in teams, often across disciplines, and 'sell' our ideas and projects to upper management.

HOW TO INFLUENCE PEOPLE AND WIN OVER ANYONE (AUDIO CD)

For just $14.97 and under an hour you can master the same Influence Skills Fortune 500 executives pay $2,000 for at all-day seminars.

Seven Secrets of Influence, the bestselling book (by Elaina Zuker) and corporate seminar has now been condensed into a valuable, user-friendly audio program.

Now, you can get this powerful information in the privacy of your home, office or car.

Coming Soon!

The newly updated version of the international bestseller *The 7 Secrets of Influence.*

How to reach us

To engage Ms. Zuker as a speaker or consultant, to book a seminar for your company or organization or to learn how to become a licensed Partner for Secrets of Influence,
visit the website at **www.ezinfluence.com**
or contact us at **ez4u@ezinfluence.com**
or by phone at **514-933-5135**

Acknowledgements

I have been the lucky recipient of many *You X 2* experiences, (i.e. the multiplication of my resources or knowledge) mostly from mentors, bosses and teachers, who instilled in me the "failure is not an option" idea, before it was a T-shirt and a corporate slogan.

Of course, I didn't know then about Peer Mentoring, or even thought much about it. Primarily, it was the idea that, with someone in my corner, someone who believed in me, I could develop self-confidence and succeed.

As Brian Schwartz of SelfPublish.org, my talented and wise colleague whose support I really value, said when he learned about the concept for my new book: "You know, sometimes I long for my high-school teacher. I work alone, and no one cares whether I tackle that next project or not. I wish I had someone to be accountable to." From the beginning of this project, he has been a great sounding board and supporter of the idea. With Brian in my corner, I have a great publishing coach by my side.

※

First, I have to acknowledge my optimistic parents, who, despite a difficult reality, always "thought positive" and taught us that every day is a fresh start. My next *You X 2* support was from Mrs. Goldberg, my home room teacher in the 9th grade, who told me to quit my back -of -the room clowning and use my good brain for schoolwork – or else! I never found out what her "or else" meant, but just one withering look from her and all my jokes fell flat.

Alec Fiorentino, my first boss in Montreal, showed me to my desk, gave me an overflowing "inbox" and left town for three days. When I started to ask him what was I to do with certain papers, he said, as he ran out the door, "you'll figure it out, Ms. Zuker." And somehow, I did! He trusted me with his important work, and I never let him down.

As a young woman, I was hired in San Francisco as the "Girl Friday" to a famous private eye, Hal Lipset. My office was in the drawing room of his 26-room Victorian mansion in Pacific Heights. While this was a great perk, I had no clue about how this business worked. The boss was always away, either out of town on cases, or doing his gumshoe work somewhere in the Bay Area. I was struggling to figure out all the office systems. I kept trying to quit, telling him this "wasn't my field." He said, "I'm successful because I have excellent judgment – you can do this job."

Ellen Jacobsen, one of my first employers in New York, was a very successful public relations woman. She hired me after a 30-minute interview, then assigned me to my first project: organizing the publicity for the launch of the Christian Dior Men's Wear Show at the Hotel Pierre in New York.

I was so new to the city I didn't even know where the Pierre was, let alone who to contact in the press. She gave me lists of things to do every day and encouraged me, and always emphasized that we could not fail! Somehow I pulled it off. She said she never doubted that I could.

Sometimes the best "boost" came from someone who believed in me enough to leave me alone in the deep end; I usually swam and didn't sink. In fact, I usually learned and grew.

One of my first consulting clients, AT & T, hired me at top dollar to conduct training programs for the thousands of women who worked there. I thought I was doing a great job.

One day at lunch the woman who had hired me looked at me, respectfully, and said, "you know, we love your seminar, our people are really learning a lot, your content is so valuable. But , for this kind of top level program, we expect your handouts and materials to be classy and first- rate." They were simply photocopied, stapled packets of notes. She didn't have to tell me this; she was trying to help me keep this important contract. She was giving me a "loving kick in the can'ts".

I hired a graphic designer the next day and poured most of my earnings into creating a beautiful set of participant materials, expensive-looking binders which were up to the standards of this world-class company and its employees.

Most of these supporters were not peers. They were far more experienced and knowledgeable than I was. They were "mentors" in the original sense. They believed in my abilities and were most generous in giving me advice and helping me build my self-confidence.

I have no idea why people believed in my abilities, when I didn't.

I first got the idea of pairing up with a peer as a mentor when my then business partner, Joan Alevras, and I made lists of our different skills and resources. We called our little company "Resources, Inc." and our mission was to help other women identify, access and use their own resources and those of others to achieve success.

We made a pact with each other to support each other in our own separate goals. We called it "Peer Mentoring". We checked in with each other to review our progress. It was comforting to have someone query me about how my efforts were going and to look at the stumbling blocks (often self-inflicted) in my way.

We even called this process "Goal Tenders." Later, I learned that the definition of the term was different than what we thought it meant, in other words, "you tend my goal and I'll tend yours". It was years later, in fact just a few months ago, that my editor, Ellen Crosby, a Canadian and a hockey fan, pointed out that a "goal tender" means just the opposite of what I thought. It means preventing someone from getting to their goal, which is the opposite of what we were trying to say!

Joan and I have gone our separate ways and I have continued to refine and practice the process we implemented. In the many training programs I conducted (on Influence Skills, Time Management, Business Writing, Team Development) I have taught participants to use the Peer Mentor process as a way to reinforce and refresh their learning from the course.

Twenty years ago, I picked up a used copy of the book "The Gift" by the famous French anthropologist, Marcel Mauss, about the intricate customs and practices of tribes and societies regarding reciprocity, potlatch, the kula and other exotic rituals. I sensed that these customs were a foundational element of the Peer Mentor process.

To my disappointment, the book, translated from the original French, was so dense and academic I couldn't follow most of it.

I kept it though, and thought that one day I would try deciphering it again. It took many years and finding the brilliant Montreal anthropologist, Dr. Gabriella Djerrahian, the author of Chapter 4 of this Book. Gaby, a fluent French speaker has read the book in its original language and was very familiar with Mauss and his seminal work. With her academic discipline, broad knowledge and beautiful writing she brought us this user-friendly understanding of Mauss' work and findings.

In addition to the chapter she wrote, Gaby has been incredibly helpful in the overall conceptual framework for the book, helping me to shape the chapters on Barter and The Sharing Economy, and to elucidate how it all ties into the new concept of Peer Mentoring.

Although she was originally hired to just write one chapter, I think of her more as a collaborator. Her knowledge, insight, enthusiasm and sheer smarts have made this project a joy to work on.

∞

When I began interviewing people to edit my manuscript, one CV stood head and shoulders above the rest. Ellen Crosby, an English Major and Graduate Student at McGill University, whose academic credentials were so impressive, complete with all the awards and distinctions (Dean's List, Awards, Scholarships) she had received. I was looking for an editor, and in addition to her academic achievements (and part time jobs to support herself) she had been an editor for several publications in her Nova Scotia hometown as well as in Montreal.

Ellen has far, far exceeded my expectations of a mere copy editor. She has challenged me on consistency, citations and all the other important details which make a tightly constructed and coherent manuscript. Her insights and focus on the big picture have been so welcomed as I struggled through every chapter. It has been a delight to work with her. Watch out world, this young woman is a force to be reckoned with!

Travers Hartnett, my good friend and fellow author (and entrepreneur and Renaissance man) has, from the beginning of this project, been a great sounding board and idea generator. When the book was a tiny seedling, Travers was already thinking outside the box and seeing the entire "garden." I'm so grateful for the gift of his time, friendship and smarts.

And last, but not least, my darling Nancy Lee Havens Vaughn Miller, who has been a dear friend and chief cheerleader for all these years. It seems like yesterday that we spent an entire day in the "Success Department" of Barnes and Noble, reviewing hundreds of titles for format, font and focus. It was clear that this was not going to be "just another self-help book."

Nancy, in her "Executive Vice President, Creative" hat, helped me shape the book within the current context of the business and life environment, helped sharpen my thinking on the audience and positioning of the book, and has been an advisor on every single phase of the process.

Finally, all my students at Montclair State University, who were the first subjects of my early experiments with Peer-Mentoring. They're all grown up and out in the world now, and I'd like to think that they took this helpful model into their careers and life, and are flourishing in whatever they've chosen to do. And that they've used the simple but powerful idea of *You X 2* to continue to expand their learning and success.

Dear reader: I hope you enjoyed
You X 2 - and plan to use some
of its ideas and techniques.

Some of our readers have purchased a second book
as a gift to their Peer Mentor, to get both of you
started on the process.

As you know, we as authors depend on reviews
(like restaurants, Uber and airbnb) from our customers/readers.

If you liked the book, and got value from reading it, would you please take a moment to post your honest review wherever you purchased the book? (Amazon, bookstore, etc.)
It would mean a lot!

Thanks so much, and
Wishing you Much Success!

Sincerely,
Elaina

Endnotes

[1] P. 4, English translation of his book *The Gift: The Form and Reason for Exchange in Archaic Societies* (1923).

[2] Particularly from Polynesia, Melanesia and the North-West of Canada and the United States, and in various civilizations (Scandinavian, Babylonian, Roman, Germanic and Indian).

[3] Risdale, Frank. 1997. A Discussion of the Potlatch and Social Structure, TOTEM : The University of Western Ontario Journal of Anthropology, Vol. 3, Issue 2, article 3.

[4] Grinde 2004.

[5] See p. 7 of the English translation of *The Gift: The Form and Reason for Exchange in Archaic Societies* (1923) for an explanation.

[6] This section is based on an article published by Andrej Rus in 2008: "'Gift vs. commodity' debate revisited," *Anthropological Notebooks*, 14 (1), pp. 81-102.

[7] Pp 84, Rus 2008.

[8] Many of the historical facts about barter described here are condensed from the the Overview in Chapter 1 of *The Complete Idiot's Guide to Barter & Trade Exchanges* by Jerry Howell and Tom Chmielewski (2009 Penguin Group).

[9] https://www.linkedin.com/pulse/how-create-influence-linkedin-keywords-beyond-elaina-zuker?trk=prof-post.

www.ingramcontent.com/pod-product-compliance
Lightning Source LLC
Chambersburg PA
CBHW070147080526
44586CB00015B/1877